JANE
AND
HENRY
A WORLD WAR II
ADVENTURE

By Rebecca Borger
Illustrated by Victoria Skakandi

Cover design by Robin Fight
Cover illustration by Victoria Skakandi
© 2021 Jenny Phillips
goodandbeautiful.com

Table of Contents

1. A Brave Adventure 1
2. Preparing a Place 9
3. Arrival at the Village School 17
4. Orchard Glen Farm 25
5. A Prayer in the Night 33
6. A Visit from Mother 47
7. Snow Surprise 60
8. A Countryside Christmas 71
9. Dunkirk Miracle 80
10. God Moves in a Mysterious Way 90
11. Goodbye for Now 100

Jane and Henry: A WWII Adventure

To Micah
Philippians 2:13–15

Jane and Henry: A WWII Adventure: A Sequel

To A & M and E,
my own dream come true
Ephesians 3:20–21

1

A Brave Adventure

September 1939

There was a whistle in the background, and Jane could see a stream of smoke curling up into the sky. She clutched Henry's hand with a fierce grip. The train was coming toward the platform. Soon, it would be time to board.

"Henry, grab your bag tightly. Don't forget your mask." Jane spoke firmly to her younger brother. It was 1939, and everyone in Britain carried a cardboard box with a gas mask. Everyone had been drilled in how to use the masks, too. The children were no exception. Jane knew how to draw hers on over her head and how to help Henry with his. She gripped his hand again. They mustn't be separated.

Mother pressed close to them. She placed her hands on their shoulders. Jane and Henry felt the love and strength in the warmth of her hands.

"Darlings, be strong," she said, as she leaned over them. She pressed her cheek to Jane's head and pulled Henry close. Father was away. A pilot with the Royal Air Force, he had already been called to war preparations at the start of it all. The children had said goodbye to him days ago. Mother was on her own.

"Can't you come, too, Mummy?" Henry asked in a small voice.

"No, darling. I can't. You know I can't just yet. I have to stay here and help the war effort in London, but I think I will be able to visit. And we can write as much as we like. Please write to me as soon as you get home with the family you will be staying with, and let me know where you are. Don't forget—our address is on this label." She touched the labels hanging around the necks of the children.

Jane pressed her lips tightly together. Her hair hung in two straight, tidy braids over her shoulders. Her gray eyes were large and fringed with long black lashes. She blinked once as though to set her mind straight.

"We will write as soon as we possibly can, Mummy." She spoke clearly. At ten, she felt responsible for seven-year-old Henry. She put her arm around him in a protecting squeeze and looked up with hope into her mother's face.

Henry leaned against Jane. His thatch of blond hair wouldn't stay straight, and his blue eyes were shining just a bit too much. Usually full of an impish twinkle, today, the blue seemed to swim. He gave a quick shrug of his shoulders and swallowed hard. Then, bravely, he smiled at Mum.

She smiled back and sighed. Then, she smoothed their hair one after the other and straightened their collars. Everywhere she looked, there were children. Jane and Henry were standing in a sea of faces. Children of all ages were bustling closer to load the train that would be arriving any minute. The smiling volunteers each had an armband around their arms, and they moved about helping children, offering drinks, and supervising the platform that was full of pent-up energy.

It was the time of the Second World War, and England was moving her children to safety.

All the children standing on the platform were being evacuated to the English countryside. They were going to leave London behind. Far from the dangers and threat of war, the children would be sheltered there. On Friday, Jane had come home from school with a notice tucked between her books. The notice urged parents to evacuate the children. The countryside was offered as an appealing adventure: it would be a holiday for Jane and Henry! It would be a holiday for the more than 800,000 children moved from England's cities to safe areas in the first days of World War II. The notice included a list of things she and Henry should pack and where they were to go. They had only a couple of days' notice to gather the items and prepare. It had been a bit of a bustle to gather everything, but somehow they managed. Mummy had worked quickly and efficiently to prepare. She would do anything to keep her mind off Father being away and the way everything was changing.

Mother had come with them to the station. She couldn't bear to send her children off without her last loving goodbye. Some children were there without their parents, shuffled together by school and grade level and led by teachers. These parents had said their goodbyes before the students had journeyed to the station, not wanting to stretch out any grief. Mummy didn't feel that way. She wanted her children to feel her courage so they would have a pattern for their own. She sheltered them now in the length of her shadow and the comfort of her presence. Jane and Henry felt her strength and stood a bit taller.

The train whooshed to a stop, and children shuffled closer.

Mother came around to face the children. She knelt down and looked them in the eye.

"It is time," she said softly. "Stay together if you can. We will write each week. I will come to visit when I am able. I will write to you and tell you of Father and the Royal Air Force." She placed a hand on each soft cheek and then drew them close. She closed her eyes at the silky touch of their hair against her cheek. Only the deep desire for their safety was strong enough to compel her to send them away into the countryside.

"Yes, Mummy." Jane spoke quietly. Her eyes glistened. Henry swallowed hard. He hugged his mother tightly.

"I will watch out for Jane," he said. "I will write." He repeated the words just spoken. Saying them made the situation seem more real and less like a dream.

Mother smiled through her tears. No more words could be said in that moment without a ghastly choking sound coming with them, so she chose instead to smile and hug the children. Then, she stood up and gently pushed the children forward so they could board the train.

It was time. It was time for them to journey to the English countryside and to safety.

Jane braced her shoulders as if to steady herself from the inside out. With Henry's hand in hers, she stepped forward and began to climb onto the train along with all the other children. Jane and Henry walked down the aisle until they found seats near a window. They pressed their faces out the window to see their mother.

She was standing on the platform with shiny eyes and a smile. She waved. Jane and Henry waved back. More and more children were climbing onto the train and getting settled.

Suddenly, the peal of a whistle resounded through the air. With a rumble and a jolt, the train slowly jerked forward. They were off. Jane squeezed Henry's hand; she was on her own now. Henry was her special charge. She wouldn't let Mummy and Father down.

2

Preparing a Place

Mary set the jug down on the counter. The fresh milk sloshed a bit, and foam bubbled along the insides of the jug. She brushed a stray strand of hair away from her face. Her cheeks were flushed pink, and bright blue eyes shone from her face. She gave a little shiver. Tonight was the night. She had been praying all day. She wiped her hands on her apron. She was gathering items for their evening meal. John was with the horses, tending

Jane and Henry: A World War II Adventure

to their needs and seeing that all was in order. He would be in soon. They would eat and then they would . . . . The door banged shut a bit, and her husband, a farmer, entered the kitchen. He grinned warmly at her, and she smiled back.

"John!" she called happily. She still loved to see his face in the doorway. It never grew old.

"The children come tonight, Mary." he said in a low rumble. They had volunteered to accept billeted children being evacuated from London. "We must head out to the village school in an hour."

"I know, John," she replied softly. The look on her face stopped him in his tracks. He crossed the kitchen over to her. He took her hand in his.

"Let us pray," he said. "Almighty Lord, we lift up all these children being brought out of London to safety. Thank You, merciful Father, for the precious gift of London's own children. Almighty Lord, You know we agree together to offer our home and our farm as a safe place for children. Help us to know which children You have matched us with. Guide us as we go tonight to bring home children to this farm. Heavenly Father, we pray, on behalf of all the children, that You will be close to them and comfort them. Help them each to know Your love and feel safe far away from their parents and the families they know. With thanks, through Jesus Christ our Lord. Amen."

Mary echoed John's "amen" in a quiet voice. She leaned her head against his shoulder. He stood with her for a moment. For years, they had longed for children. Unable to have their own, Mary felt a bit nervous but also excited at the thought of opening their home to the evacuees. She knew she would be opening her heart, too. She had been praying for the children every day. She wanted to show them God's love and give them all the solid goodness of the English countryside.

John squeezed her hand. He knew what children meant to Mary; he knew what they meant to him. This would be an adventure. It could be a trial, too. Hopefully, the farm would be a safe place full of love for children who were being displaced because of the threat of danger.

"Let's have tea; we can set some aside for the children. I am sure they'll be hungry! Then, we can load up to head to town." Mary bustled about setting out food and place settings. She placed two additional plates and cups on the table. They had agreed to take two children at this time. It was hard to imagine their little faces sitting at this table, but soon it would be so.

The tea was hot, and the biscuits were perfect with the home-churned butter. A spot of fresh cream was just the ticket. Mary and John ate heartily and quietly. Their thoughts were occupied with the change coming their way. Mary had placed a candle in the center of the table. A sprig of greenery and several of her own favorite roses added a touch of color. She planned to feed the children all the farm-fresh eggs and milk they could stomach. She smiled at the thought. War rations and food shortages were far from her mind.

Everything was just beginning, and they were deep in the English countryside. For them, air raids and bombs would always be a distant threat. But Mary didn't know this yet; she didn't know anything about it other than the urgent need to rehome thousands of children. She and John were more than willing to do their part and extend an open door to children in need.

The cuckoo clock in the living room called half-past 5 p.m. The children had been traveling all day. It was almost time to go.

"I'm just going to run up and look over their rooms one more time," said Mary. She had laid out fresh linens and water basins. She ran up the stairs and peeked into the rooms. Walking across the hardwood floors, she fluffed pillows and straightened bedding. The windows looked out over the orchards.

"The view will do them good," she said quietly, taking in the rolling English countryside stretching far into the distance. Quietly, she bowed her head and prayed, silently. She prayed carefully and distinctly, each word coming from her heart with faith and love. With a last glance at the well-tended rooms, Mary hurried back down the stairs to John.

Together, they went out to hook horses to the cart. Two shiny brown horses stood at attention, snorting a bit. John stroked their heads fondly. Chester and Ginger were their names, and they were gentle and good. Mary loved a ride with them at the lead. Climbing in, John grabbed the reins and called to the horses to begin; with a gentle bump, the cart rolled forward, and they began the journey to greet the children. All over England children were gathering at central locations after long train rides. In some villages it was the local schoolhouse, in others they were gathered at the village hall. Mary and John were headed to the schoolhouse, the central gathering location for their village. It was a treat to be out with John in the evening air with the gentle team rocking them forward and onward. She leaned next to John. A breeze lifted the gold hair against her face. John smiled. So much unknown and so much anticipation, it almost sparked in the air. The ride to the village school was quick. The children would have to walk every day once they began school. The village had already begun preparations to welcome all the new children into their schoolhouse and lessons. The schoolyard was well lit, and people were milling about and heading inside. John and Mary gripped hands tightly together in an unspoken prayer. Then, they stepped down and went to enter the school.

3

Arrival at the Village School

With a long jolt and a shooting plume of steam, the train pulled into the station. Jane and Henry had spent one very long day in rail travel. Traveling for hours and hours, they had just pulled into the station and were getting off in order to be shuttled to the village school. Their sandwiches were long gone; they were so thirsty, their tongues felt dry. Teachers and volunteers were bustling them forward.

"Come on, Henry. Stay with me." Jane pressed Henry forward and then hurried to grab his hand as they stepped onto the platform. Escorted by adults, they went to get on the bus. Crunched in with loads of other children, exhausted and weary, Jane could hardly think straight. It was all she could do to keep her wits about her. Henry leaned against her, his blond hair a shock of brightness against her dark coat. Jane closed her eyes and thought of Mother and Daddy, each giving their best for the war effort. She wanted to give her best, too. She clutched their parcels against her lap, holding Henry's for him while balancing hers as well.

The ride on the bus was bumpy. All the children were edgy. The long day of travel and the time away from family was fraying the best resolve. Jane knew they just needed to hold on a little longer. She let Henry rest against her. Finally, they were at the village school.

The adults helped them off the bus. They climbed down to walk toward the school. Stepping inside, they saw a room full of activity. Grown-ups who had agreed to foster children; adult volunteers; weary, exhausted, and dirty children; and the billeting officer were crowded together trying to get situated. The billeting officer had a frazzled appearance with a clipboard in hand and a furrowed brow. There were so many children to sort. He lined the children up against the wall. The room was full of adults ready to receive children. Jane realized they were choosing children one by one. She squeezed closer to Henry. They must stay together! Henry leaned against her, trying to blend into her side.

Mary and John were among the crowd of adults. They were looking over all the children. Mary had a hard knot in her belly. How would she know which children to choose? They were hoping and planning for two. The children all looked scared. Her belly flopped. These poor children! John was behind her; his taller and wider frame filled the space. He was also looking over the line of children. He was a comforting strength behind her, and Mary took a shaky breath.

"Look, Mary!" John whispered urgently. He was angled toward Jane and Henry. "Do you see the small girl with the braids and the little boy next to her?" He was leaning against Mary; his breath was hot against her ear.

"Oh, John! Let's see if we can get them," Mary answered back and started toward the billeting officer.

"Sir, sir—please, we'd like to take that boy and girl." Mary was speaking, and John was pointing gently. "We'll take them." Mary and John spoke together and then looked at each other and smiled. The billeting officer looked at Mary and John, and then he looked at Henry and Jane. He moved over to them and took hold of the tags around their necks.

"This is Jane, and this is Henry. They are from London. Sister and brother?" He raised an eyebrow as he looked at their dirty faces.

"Yes, sir," Jane answered politely.

"Alright," the billeting officer said as he gently nudged the children toward the couple. "Off you go!" he added with a bit of a lilt in his voice. It was a good feeling to have children matched to a home, and two at once to boot! He gave a bit of a relieved smile and then was swept into the bustle and crowd, on to the need at hand.

Mary leaned down to look at the children face-to-face. "Hullo, there," she said gently. "I'm Mary

Stuart. Please call me Aunt Mary. We are so glad to have you," she added with warmth.

"And I'm John," the tall farmer broke in. "Call me Uncle John. We've been waiting for you."

Jane felt overwhelmed. Everything was strange. John and Mary had a twang and a roll in their words that was so different from her own London accent. The kindness in the couple's voices brought quick tears to her eyes. She blinked them back hard. Henry gripped her hand with a fierce, damp squeeze. He was hanging on for life. Jane looked down at Henry. He looked so small and bewildered. She squared her shoulders and looked up into the faces of this new couple.

"Thank you. We are Jane and Henry Townsend." She offered these words primly with brave politeness. Henry rubbed his fist across his grubby face. Then, he remembered his manners and thrust out his hand.

"How do you do? I'm Henry," he offered with manly effort.

Arrival at the Village School

John took his hand carefully. "Nice to meet you, Henry," he answered gravely. Then, John cleared his throat. The displaced children tore at his heart. With a quick blink and a cough, he turned to look at Mary. She smiled at him with her heart in her eyes.

"Let's get you home, Jane and Henry," he said as Mary put her arm around them and gently urged them forward. They stepped out into the cool night air. Jane looked up into the darkest sky she had ever seen. The stars spangled the sky like glitter, more than she had ever seen before in all her ten years of life. The country air was ripe and fresh. Jane took a deep, deep breath. Mary helped them walk quickly toward the cart and horses. They climbed in, and she tucked them round with a warm, coarse blanket.

"There, now. That'll keep you warm as we head back to the farm. I'm sure you're just all tired out." She comforted in soothing tones as she settled them neatly into their spots.

Henry and Jane were speechless—so tired, hungry, and thirsty—they didn't have any words to offer. John and Mary didn't seem to expect any, so that, at least, was a relief.

John grabbed hold of the reins and clucked to Chester and Ginger. With a forward jolt, they were off, down the rough road, heading into a new and unknown life—together.

4

Orchard Glen Farm

Jane stepped unsteadily out of the cart as the horses waited for everyone to exit. She stood blinking in the darkness. Holding out her hand, she felt for Henry as he swayed next to her. She could make out the dark outline of the house just in front of them.

"There we are!" called John. "I'll just tend to the horses." And he began leading the horses toward the barn. Mary stepped closer to the children. With a soft and gentle voice, she greeted them once more.

"Here, now. We've just got to step ahead. I'm so glad to welcome you to our home. Just inside now, and I'll fix you tea."

Mary led the way for the children, and they crunched on the pebbled walkway as they moved to the house.

Henry and Jane stepped inside the house after Mary. They entered a tidy, well-furnished farmhouse and followed her through to the kitchen.

"There's a washbasin over there." Mary pointed toward the washroom. The children went over to scrub their hands. Mary set out bread and butter, fresh milk, jam, and cold slices of ham. She put the kettle on for hot tea.

"Now then, you must be hungry," she said to the children. They looked a bit stunned as they stood waiting, unsure what to do next. "Come. Come and sit down," she urged warmly.

Jane took a seat at the tidy kitchen table, and Henry climbed up onto a chair next to her.

"Thank you, Aunt . . . Mary." Jane managed to work the unfamiliar name around her tongue. Mary smiled gently. Henry was waiting patiently. Mary lit another lamp to add more light to the dim room. She sliced bread and placed it on the children's plates. She poured milk for each. She looked at each child carefully.

"Uncle John and I are so glad you are here. We have been praying for a way to help the war effort and the children, what with the farmers being exempt from the war effort on the front lines and all." Jane and Henry nodded. They knew that there were rules about who could join the army or air force and serve in the military. Farmers were highly needed at home to keep up industry to support the war effort through their crops and stock. Mary would never speak out loud the relief she felt at John's reprieve from battle; it was something she clutched to her heart in quiet gratitude.

"I want you to go ahead and eat, but first, let me pray and say a blessing. We thank the Lord before we eat here, and I am going to thank Him for your safe arrival, too," she continued, her soft voice soothing the children. They felt a bit odd. No one ever prayed before meals at home, but Mum had trained them well in their manners. Jane nodded politely. Henry looked at her and quickly nodded, too. Mary smiled.

"Almighty Lord, thank You for the safe arrival of Jane and Henry Townsend. Thank You that John

and I can open our home and welcome them here for safety and protection. Bless them, Almighty God, Giver of good things, as they eat this food and in all the days they spend here with us at Orchard Glen Farm. Most of all, Heavenly Father, help them to know Your love. Through Jesus Christ our Lord, I pray. Amen."

As Mary finished her prayer, she looked up at the children. They opened their eyes slowly. She took a piece of bread in hand and covered it with a bit of jam. As she got ready to take the first bite, the children knew they could do so, too. They tucked into the food with gusto. They drained their cups to the bottom, and Mary filled them again and then again.

"The lav is outside, back of the kitchen," she said kindly, realizing that the children would probably need to use it soon, if not already. "I'll show you as soon as you are done eating."

An outdoor bathroom was a new experience for Jane and Henry, who had the luxury of indoor plumbing in London. "There will be a lot to get used to in the country, that's for sure," Jane thought.

Mary led the children out a back door and down a neatly trimmed garden walk. There was the outhouse, and Jane and Henry had yet another new experience on this bewildering day of all things new. Thankfully, the outhouse was spotless and fresh, with the sharp bite of disinfectant in the air. Soon the children were standing once more on the garden walk, feeling much more comfortable. Aunt Mary smiled down at them. They were such small sprites with such strong spirits, especially Jane, who mothered Henry with a skill delightful to watch.

"Come, I'll help you get settled in your rooms, and in the morning we can send a letter right off to your mummy so that she will know you have arrived safely and where she can reach you."

"Thank you, Aunt Mary," Henry said, looking up at her with hope in his eyes.

They walked back to the kitchen and found John there washing up. He grinned as they entered through the door. "Good to see you!" he called merrily.

"I'm just going to take the children up, John, dear," Mary replied. "They are tuckered out."

"Yes, indeed," John answered. "I can see that. Good night, Jane. Good night, Henry," John called cheerfully.

"Good night!" both children answered obediently, so tired they could scarcely walk. Mary helped them up the stairs and into their rooms. Quickly, they washed their faces and changed clothing. Mary made sure to tuck them into bed under the handmade quilts crafted by her family for generations. The soft cotton and beautiful colors draped over the children like a warm hug.

Everything was clean and fresh, and Jane's eyes were closing the minute she lay down on the firm bed. Mary placed their clothing and parcels neatly together in their rooms. They would need their address tags in the morning. She didn't want them to feel confused when they woke up.

Saying one last quiet prayer as she held the lamp in her hand, she looked over the children with a protective eye. All was well, so she headed downstairs. Tomorrow would soon be at hand, with more all-new experiences for these two.

5

A Prayer in the Night

A bright beam of sunlight danced across Jane's face, and she woke up, scrunching her eyes tight and blinking against the morning light.

"Moooo! Moooo!" A cow lowed right outside her window. She sat up in surprise. Where was she? She couldn't remember anything. Her heart pounded in her chest as she tried to figure it out. Suddenly, a pajama-clad bundle leaped into bed next to her and buried his blond head in her pillow.

"Henry!" she cried out. "What are you doing?" Henry peered up at her with glimmering blue eyes. He didn't say a word.

"Come on," she continued, "up you go! Let's get ready for the day. It's our first day on the farm." She gently pushed him off the bed and climbed out herself.

The two siblings quickly dressed and washed. Together, they headed down the stairs. There was a delicious smell of sausage in the air. They could hear singing coming from the kitchen. They didn't recognize the tune. Mary was wearing a bright white apron and working, with energy, in the kitchen.

"Good morning!" she called to the children as they entered the kitchen. "So glad to see the two of you this morning." A smile stretched across her face.

"Good morning, ma'am," Henry uttered respectfully.

"Oh please, my dears, call me Aunt Mary as I told you last night—but no wonder if you didn't remember. Such a tiring journey you had!"

A small smile of relief and ease stretched across Jane's face, and she took a breath. Wonder of wonders! Perhaps this evacuation adventure would be a happy one after all. She stood up a bit taller.

"Can we help you, Miss?" Jane paused and then tried again. "I mean, can we help you, Aunt Mary?" she asked.

"I would greatly appreciate having you children help with the setting of the table for our meals and the washing up of dishes afterward," Mary said warmly. Then, she stopped to look at the children to see what response they would have to the duties she suggested.

"We would be glad to help," Jane said firmly.

"I think Uncle John could use some help around the farm as well. Perhaps you can gather the eggs each morning, for one. There will also be work in the gardens." Mary sighed a bit.

"We're happy to help just like Jane said," Henry offered stoutly.

"My, that's a blessing!" Aunt Mary grinned with

relief. "Let's start with the table and have a bite to eat first." The children helped to set the table, and in what seemed like moments, they sat down to eat the tasty breakfast.

"Goodness," Jane thought to herself, "I've never tasted such delicious food before in my life." Her eyes opened wide. Country living! So different from London. Jane and Henry tucked away as much food as their hungry bellies could hold. Mary was as pleased as could be to see their hearty appetites. She hoped it meant they would adjust quickly to their time on the farm, away from their London home. Henry had some juice trickling down his chin; he quickly swiped at it with a napkin.

"Why don't you children write a letter to your Mummy to let her know where you are as soon as dishes are washed?" Mary suggested. "We should get that to the post first thing." After they washed the dishes, she set the children up at the table with sharpened pencils and helped them fill out the address of their new home at Orchard Glen Farm.

Jane's note said,

Dear Mummy,

I am glad to tell you that we have safely arrived. Henry and I are together, and all is well. We are staying with a kind couple in the countryside on a farm called Orchard Glen. Please write soon, Mummy, and give my love to Daddy. The return address on the postcard is our location. I hope we get to see you soon!

Love,
Jane

Henry's note said,

Dear Mummy,

Jane and I are here at Orchard Glen Farm. We are fine. The sausages are first-rate. Please write soon. I miss you! I miss Daddy!

Love,
Henry

"Nicely done," said Mary when the children had finished and checked for spelling and tidy writing. "I'll have John get these to the post. I am going to jot a note off to your mum myself and let her know she is always welcome here. Your dad is in the Royal Air Force?" Mary ended with a question.

"Yes," Jane replied quietly.

"Well, that's just fine. We'll be sure to pray for him every day and thank God for his service to our country," Mary replied. Jane wondered if she would get used to all this praying over everything. At home they never prayed. She mulled it over in her mind. She was glad Mary cared enough to pray for Daddy. "Go on out to find John in the barn. I'll just get this letter done. See if you can gather some eggs." Mary nodded toward the kitchen door. She sat down to draft her letter, and the children headed outside.

The warm sunshine hit them full in the face as they stepped outside, and the sounds of the countryside filled the air. The sky was a perfect blue. A gentle busyness filled the air. Jane looked to the orchard on her left. The barn was straight ahead, past the neat cottage garden and the outhouse. They walked forward and found John cleaning out stalls.

"Good morning!" he called as the children entered.

"Hullo, Uncle John," Jane called with more confidence. Mary's warmth had eased some of the uncomfortable newness of everything. "We've come to see about some eggs."

"Ah, yes!" John put down his pitchfork. "Come with me." He led the children to the henhouse and showed them how to find the eggs tucked in the nests. "It's best to gather the eggs when the chickens are out to scratch," he told the children. "Otherwise, they might peck at your wee hands when you reach in their nests." Henry watched, wide-eyed. "The baskets for collecting eggs are back in the barn. Come with me, and you can gather for Aunt Mary."

John helped the children locate the baskets and showed them how to store them back in the right place when they were done. With a basket on each arm, Jane and Henry went back to the henhouse and collected eggs for the very first time. Henry had to be extra careful not to be too rough—a gentle hand was needed with the fragile eggs.

The first day on the farm was full of new life. The cows with their solemn, deep eyes blinked at the children; there were ducks quacking and waddling about. Chester and Ginger, the beautiful cart horses, tickled their palms as the children fed them apples provided by Mary. The very air smelled different: pungent and fresh. Pansies, forget-me-nots, and red clover grew everywhere. Jane and Henry also wandered into Mary's own prize rose garden. It was clear Mary took time and care in this much-loved place. Many gorgeous varieties of English roses were arranged artfully, growing with healthy luxuriance. Jane wandered about filled with wonder. The lovely fragrance danced on the gentle wind, and the petals felt like silk. By the end of the day, Jane and Henry knew all the animals, had helped Uncle John with many chores new to them,

A Prayer in the Night

and had enjoyed farm-fresh food at the table, which they had neatly set themselves.

Late that night, Jane woke to muffled crying. It was Henry. She sat up, wide-eyed. The whole house was pitch black. She had to get to him. Carefully, she slipped out of bed. Feeling with careful hands, she made her way to his bedroom.

"Henry!" she whispered urgently. "Henry!" He had his face pressed deep into his pillow, and he was crying hard. Jane carefully felt her way over to his bed. She climbed in next to him.

"Henry, I'm here," she whispered. Henry snuffled into her arm. "What is it?" Jane continued.

"I miss Mummy. I'm scared for Daddy." Henry gasped out the words between choked sobs.

"I know. Me, too," Jane said. She didn't know what else to say, but she knew she had to be strong for Henry. Suddenly there was a creak on the floor and a glimmer of light. Then, Mary appeared, clutching a candle in one hand, its beam shining on her face. She peered into the bedroom.

"Everything alright?" she asked gently.

"Yes, ma'am," Jane replied. "I just came to check on Henry." She didn't want Mary to know how hard Henry had been crying or that they both were afraid in the night.

Mary walked carefully into the room. She placed the candle down on the nearby table stand. She sat quietly on the edge of the bed. Despite great effort, Henry's shaky breaths still hung heavy in the dark night air.

"It's a scary time, no doubt," Mary said. "Leaving everything you know far behind—and all the danger of the war at hand. It's natural to be afraid, and it's natural to be lonesome and scared." Jane and Henry lay in the dark listening to her voice. "I know Orchard Glen Farm is nothing like your home, but I want you to always remember how glad Uncle John and I are to have you here. We haven't had children of our own, and we are so blessed to have you both here for this time. Let's say a prayer for your family."

Mary placed her hands on the children's heads.

They felt kindness in her touch.

"Merciful Lord," she prayed, "please let Jane and Henry feel Your comfort during this scary time. Help them to look to You for love and strength. Let Your comfort and peace be with us all. Thank You that You promise us supernatural peace, and we have it through You, in Jesus Christ our Lord."

Henry gave a little sigh as Mary finished. He squeezed his eyes shut tight. He squeezed Jane's hand, too.

"Jane, do you need help getting back to your room?" Mary asked kindly.

"If you please, Aunt Mary, I would like to talk to Henry for just a bit more. I can make my way back."

Aunt Mary smiled in the dark. These two were plucky friends, she could tell that. "Of course. I will see you in the morning. Don't be afraid to come for me if you are scared again or you need help," she said. She left the room as quietly as she had arrived, taking the glimmering candle with her on her way out.

"Henry," Jane whispered. "Are you alright?"

"Yes," Henry mumbled. "She prays all the time, doesn't she?" he questioned.

"She does. She is always talking about God's love," Jane answered.

"God's love . . ." Henry muttered.

"Do you think you can sleep now?" Jane asked. Henry snuggled deeper into the covers, and Jane tucked him in a bit. He yawned, and she felt the movement in the darkness. She lay next to him until she felt his breathing become gentle and more regular.

Jane lay in the dark staring at a ceiling she couldn't see. She missed Mum. Dad was far away flying a plane, possibly in danger. Who was this loving God Aunt Mary was talking about so many times each day? She couldn't understand any of it, but Aunt Mary was so kind, and for that, she was glad. Mum had taught her to be respectful of people and their beliefs. Aunt Mary seemed to walk in a kind of glowing light. Her smile, her hugs, her warm words, they all wrapped around her like a beautiful and mysterious song she wanted to understand. Jane crept out of Henry's bed and felt her way carefully back to her own. She snuggled down into her covers with Aunt Mary's words still singing in her ears about a God full of comfort and peace, a God who loves and gives strength. Jane yawned, and then suddenly she couldn't stay awake any longer. She was asleep under the eaves of Orchard Glen Farmhouse, held in God's love, although she didn't fully know it . . . yet.

6

A Visit from Mother

One night, a few weeks later, Mary and John, with Jane and Henry, were gathering in the living room just like they did every night. Jane was helping Mary place the blackout panels in all the windows. Just before they had arrived at Orchard Glen Farm, orders had come for all of England to follow "total blackout" regulations. This meant that everyone everywhere had to shut out all light from any windows with black fabric or paper to protect from enemy aircraft unleashing bombs. They always began by lighting candles so that when the fabric was in place, they would be greeted by dancing golden light. The flickering candlelight felt joyful and festive. It helped chase away any fear. Mary was singing, as she always did while she worked, and the joyful, soothing songs helped steady Jane's heart. It was always hard not to think of Father, who could be flying above the skies in battle at any moment. Mary's gentle joy helped keep the blackout regulations, which would last for the entire length of the war, from closing in on them all with a grip of anxiety.

Uncle John had a fire crackling in the fireplace to push away the damp evening air. Jane and Henry were getting used to the way Mary and John began and ended each day with prayer. Both children started to feel a comfort and a hope from the faith-filled words and scripture verses John and Mary would share with them naturally throughout their conversation. They didn't know that every night, John and Mary knelt together before bed, clasping hands and asking God to shine the light of His love in their hearts and in the hearts of Mum and Daddy. They didn't know that every night they asked God to protect their parents—Mum in London and Daddy in the air and on land at the forefront of the coming battles. But what they didn't know, they could feel: there was a protective hug around them everywhere they went at Orchard Glen Farm, and it kept darkness away.

"Well, let's turn on the wireless," John remarked as he walked over and twisted the knobs. He had laid a harness on the table to mend. The fire crackled and popped. Jane had a bit of knitting in her lap. Mary had taught her to knit and purl, and she was hard at work on her first project: a scarf for Daddy. Henry had a bit of carving at hand—the delight of a seven-year-old (almost eight-year-old) boy's heart, especially because John was a patient teacher. Mary was sewing. She was working hard to help the war effort in her own way.

Jane and Henry: A World War II Adventure

A Visit from Mother

The static crackled in the air as the station came into play. News of the war came over the airwaves. It was September 27, 1939. Poland surrendered to Germany. So far, none of the bombing raids expected in London had happened. John, Mary, Jane, and Henry listened carefully to all the news.

Mary looked at the children. "Now, I have some exciting news for you two." She smiled at their small, freckled faces. "The local school has finally managed to organize classes to include the evacuees. You will start on Monday. I also had a confirmation from your mummy. She's coming to visit on Saturday." Jane and Henry sat up a bit straighter. This was news! "Your mummy will arrive on the morning train. John will drive out to meet her. You children may go along. You will have to wake very early! I will help you get all set for school on Monday. It is a nice walk to the schoolhouse."

"Oh! We want to go meet Mummy, don't we, Henry?" Jane cried. Henry nodded. "We'll wake early!" Mummy and school! The children felt excited.

Saturday arrived, and Aunt Mary woke them while it was still dark. There was a chill in the air, and the children hurried down to the warm kitchen to eat a bite before loading up with Uncle John. Aunt Mary had hot toast and jam ready with farm-fresh eggs warm and steaming. Uncle John came in, stamping his feet and blowing on his hands.

"It's time to load up! Let's head out," he called. Jane and Henry hurried to clear the table.

"I'll wash up for you this morning," Mary said with a smile. "You have to hurry on to get Mummy." Jane looked up at her with surprise.

"Thank you, Aunt Mary," she said. "Thank you for doing the work for us." Mary smiled even more.

"God's blessings on your travel. I look forward to meeting your mum!" she said with joy.

Jane and Henry hurried to get ready and headed out to load up. Uncle John helped the children into the cart. For the journey there, he placed the children right next to him in the front. He called

A Visit from Mother

to the horses, and the cart jolted forward. Jane and Henry were shivering with anticipation.

"Would you like to drive the horses?" John asked Henry, who was sitting right next to him. Henry looked up at him with astonishment.

"Y-yes!" Henry exclaimed. His eyes were round as saucers and his blond hair was an unruly thatch springing up all over his head. John handed him the reins, and Henry's chest puffed out with the pride of responsibility. He was driving the horses! Jane bit her lips together. She was a bit nervous with Henry at the reins, but she wouldn't say anything for the world. It would ruin his joy.

After a while, John took the reins back and urged the horses into a quicker trot. They had a long journey and must hurry on to the station. The drive was full of delight. The beautiful English countryside spun by as they trotted along. Occasionally, John would sing in a low rumble. Both he and Mary loved the beautiful hymns of the Church of England. Almost under his breath, John was singing as they traveled on, and the words were from "God Moves in a Mysterious Way":

God moves in a mysterious way,
His wonders to perform;
He plants His footsteps in the sea,
And rides upon the storm.
Deep in unfathomable mines
Of never failing skill;
He treasures up His bright designs,
And works His sovereign will.
Ye fearful saints fresh courage take,
The clouds ye so much dread
Are big with mercy, and shall break
In blessings on your head.

"Blessings on your head," Jane thought to herself. She didn't quite understand, but it seemed like maybe God had a beautiful plan that she couldn't quite see just yet. Maybe God was good and kind and cared about her and Henry. Could it be? She was listening and thinking. And oh! She did need courage. Jane gripped Henry's hand for a moment.

A Visit from Mother

She couldn't wait to see Mummy!

They made it just as the train was squealing into the station. And then there she was! Mother, quickly stepping down off the train, her eyes scanning the platform, looking . . . looking. Suddenly, a smile like a sunrise split across her face and her arms were out; she had found them. She was striding quickly toward them with open arms. The children couldn't contain themselves. They took off at a quick run, and in a minute, they were in her arms. John hung back, waiting and watching. His great heart was so glad for the children in this moment, and he stood silent as a statue and watched.

Mother had the children squeezed in her arms; she couldn't hold on tight enough. Then, she knelt down and looked them in the eye.

"Oh, I've missed you both!" she said with a glimmer in her eye. Jane looked at her straight on. Her clear, gray eyes were unwavering. Henry was ready to spring from the power of his energetic joy.

His blue eyes danced, and he bounced about on his tiptoes. How glad they were to be together! Mummy stood and turned to John. She held out her hand.

"How do you do? I'm Helen Townsend," she said.

"Wonderful to meet you, ma'am. I'm John Stuart of Orchard Glen Farm. It's been wonderful having the children with us these past weeks." John smiled. "Let's get settled into the cart; it's a bit of a journey back to the farm. Do you have a trunk?"

"Just this satchel." Mother lifted the bag she was holding. She would be staying overnight because the journey was quite long from London to Orchard Glen Farm.

"Alright, then," John said, and in just a few minutes, they were loaded and journeying back to the farm. Mary had packed a cold lunch, and before long, Jane helped hand out apples and chunky sandwiches all round. It was good to eat in the fresh English air.

Mummy asked John all about Orchard Glen Farm and how it had been with the children. Were

A Visit from Mother

they well behaved? Was it a trouble? How were they settling in? John answered everything in his low, cheerful rumble. The children were a blessing; they were mighty helpful. He hoped they felt warm and welcome. It was wonderful having them at Orchard Glen Farm. He told her all about the farm and the animals, the gardens, and the orchards. Mother listened intently.

"Father is doing well," she said to the children after a time and when all her questions were satisfied. "I've brought a letter for you that we can share later."

"Oh, how lovely!" Jane breathed. Her eyes were shining. It was so sweet to have Mother with them and to hear from Father, too. She felt full to the brim with happiness.

"Mummy, we're to start school on Monday," Jane said after a while.

"Well, that's good to hear!" Mother replied. "It's important to keep up your education. The children in London are leaving school at fourteen and heading to work in the factories for the war effort. Hopefully, this war will end quickly and everyone can get back to normal life." She sighed a little. It was an uncertain time.

Finally, they arrived back at the farm. Mary was waiting with refreshment at hand. She came out to greet them and took Mrs. Townsend's hand in hers.

"So good to have you here, ma'am," she said. "I've looked forward to this for so long. Come, you must be exhausted. Just step inside, and I'll show you where to wash up. Jane or Henry can show you the lav if needed. It's just over there down the garden path." She gestured with her arm. "Everything is just this way." Mary bustled them in through the kitchen door.

"Please call me Helen," Mother said. She took a deep breath. In a way, she felt like everything was going to be alright.

The visit with Mother was wonderful. There were promises to come again. Mother thought she might be able to come once or twice a month and stay overnight. The Stuarts were so lovely and welcoming. She asked if they were sure she wouldn't be a problem, to which, of course, they reassured her that she wouldn't at all be a bother and of how glad they were that the Lord had brought them all together during these troublesome times. It was hard to say goodbye again. Jane had to muster all of her courage to keep from crying pitifully. Henry swallowed hard. He couldn't say anything at all.

In the back of their minds, they knew that the next day was the start of something new: school. Mother had managed to bring them some fresh clothes and shoes. Later that night, after Mother had been dropped back at the station and the whole house was cloaked in darkness, Jane lay again looking up at the ceiling. School. In a new place. Her belly flopped with butterflies of nervousness. It was up to her to help Henry make Mummy and Dad proud. Together, they would do their part for Britain and their family and the war.

7

Snow Surprise

December 1939

Jane quickly settled into her new school routine. Every morning, she helped with washing up and fetching eggs. Henry set the table. He helped John in the barn in the mornings, cleaning stalls and feeding animals. Jane made sure Henry had what he needed and didn't forget his lunch and then off they went for the mile walk to the village school. They had quickly settled in to classrooms with other village children and billeted evacuees. The lessons were a bit different, that was for sure. But there were friendly faces among the children, and Jane tried her best to keep her end up in mathematics and reading. She tried to keep Henry on task, too.

Among the villagers, there was talk of children heading back to London by Christmas. Not much had happened, and the anticipated London bombings hadn't occurred, yet the government was insisting parents keep their children in the countryside. There were posters put up everywhere with mottos and words to encourage families to keep their children safe and out of harm's way. Mother had already decided Jane and Henry were going to stay put. No use bringing them into possible danger only to have to move them out again. Plus, there was no guarantee they would end up back with the Stuarts if they did come back to London only to evacuate once more. She had asked Father for advice, and he agreed. Let the children stay with the Stuarts. They were safe and well cared for, and this war was unpredictable. Daddy didn't trust the calm. John and Mary were delighted. Jane and Henry already had made their own special place in each of their hearts. Hosting the children had been one real, good gift from the difficulty and uncertainty of the war.

Jane and Henry were glad to live at Orchard Glen Farm. Their days were filled with so many new experiences and so many things to learn. They loved Mummy's letters and visits. Father wrote, too, but not as often. Jane knew Mummy was working so hard for the war effort in London. She missed her so, but it gave Mummy peace of mind to know that she and Henry were a whole day's train journey from danger.

One morning, Jane woke up early to a freezing chill in the air and everything muffled as though cotton were flung over the world. She jumped out of bed, dancing in the cold, to peer out the window and saw the farm and orchards covered in a thick layer of snow. There would be no school today; the snow lay in such a thick layer over everything. Jane was so excited! It was her first snow on the farm.

"Oh, snow," she breathed with glee. Quickly, she pulled on woollen stockings and her heavy sweater. It was so close to Christmas, and the Stuarts celebrated the season with joy. Mary had decorated the house with greenery and extra candles. She had helped Jane and Henry make paper chains and pin them up all over the living room and even some in their bedrooms. There was a pageant being prepared at school. Both Jane and Henry had a speaking part. Mother was coming soon to stay for a week. She would be there on Christmas morning. John and Mary wouldn't stand for the thought that she remain alone in London with Father off at war and the children on the farm. They insisted she join them for an English countryside Christmas. Jane couldn't wait for her to arrive! Truth be told, Mother could hardly fathom the generosity and kindness of the Stuarts. Every time she visited, they showered her with warmth and love. Shyly, she accepted their prayers. She tried to bring gifts and news from

London to reciprocate their giving.

Jane was hurrying across the hall to Henry when she found he was already downstairs. Quickly, she hurried down the stairs; she heard happy chatter coming from the kitchen. Henry's voice was pitched high with excitement.

"Jane!" he cried as she entered the room. "You'll never believe it. Uncle John has built us a sled! And he's going to take us out to the best hill after breakfast." John was standing in the kitchen next to Mary with a smile spread across his face.

"Oh my," Jane said. She was speechless. She had never been sledding before.

"I've got extra mittens and scarves for you," Mary was saying, "and warm hats. Let's get our morning work done and then off you can go!"

The children hurried as fast as they could to get all the work done. Mary had to call Henry back to redo his efforts two separate times. Shoddy work was not accepted at Orchard Glen Farm. Mary was kind but firm. No use doing the work if it wasn't done well. Sheepishly, Henry came back again and then again. In the end, Jane helped him finish up so they could get out to sled together faster.

John knew the perfect sledding hill. It was a place familiar to all the village, and as they approached, they could see lots of other people out to enjoy the fresh snow and the crisp day. They trudged through the snow. John had the sled pulling behind with the steering ropes in hand. Jane's cheeks were rosy and tingling. Inside, a bubble of joy was floating all through her middle. Henry was trudging along next to John; one small hand was clutched in John's large one.

"There we are now," John said as they finally made it to the top of the hill. Jane and Henry saw Harriet and Louie, two children they knew from school.

"Hullo, Jane!" Harriet called. Her golden hair was wisping all round her face. She was bundled from head to toe. "We're about to go. Watch!" she cried out to the children as she situated herself on her sled with another chum from school, Tory. The children were off down the hill in a puff of snow.

"Oh! Yippee!" Henry squealed. He was bouncing with excitement.

"Alright!" John said with a laugh. He helped Jane and Henry sit on the sled. "I'm going to give you a good push. When you get to the bottom, tote the sled back up, and you can have a go again." Henry was in front, and John showed him how to pull the sled ropes to steer. Jane held on tight to the sides of the wooden sled. John gave a great heave, and they were off!

The air was icy cold in their faces, and they both shrieked with joy! What fun to fly down the hill! Down, down they went, ending in a puff of snow in the bank at the bottom. They rolled off the sled laughing. Little Louie was there getting ready to pull his sled back up the hill.

"Great fun, isn't it?" he asked with a little chuckle. Everyone felt carefree for just a brief moment. The fear of war was far away, and that

Snow Surprise

was just as it should be for children on a day full of snowfall and sledding.

Jane and Henry pulled their sled up the hill again and again. John gave them speed tips and steering tips. The children out for sledding that day would meet up for brief moments at the bottom of the great hill, talking about the speed of their run, the near crash they almost had, or the way that this time down was better than before. Too soon, the light began to change, and it was time to head home for evening chores, the evening meal, and gathering round the fire in the living room.

"I'll see you at school, Harriet!" Jane called as they started to head back.

"Bye, Louie!" Henry called, too.

The children waved goodbye with glad calls as they all went their separate ways.

Mary hung their wet clothing by the fire to dry. Later that night, after Jane and Henry were tucked into bed, having had the now familiar nightly prayer and blessing spoken over them, Mary found

John sitting and staring at the fire.

"Hullo, Love. Are you okay?" she asked quietly. She brought a warm cup of tea over to him. It had been a long day out in the cold, with farm chores made more challenging in the snow and the eventful sledding.

"Ah, Mary." John's shoulders slumped. "You should've seen 'em today. The joy on the sled! There's nothin' like it." Mary sat down next to him. She leaned her head against his shoulder. John put his face in his hands. Mary put her arm around him.

"It's hard to imagine what it was like without 'em," she said softly. "The Lord heard our prayers when we asked Him. He'll hear us now," she whispered. Mary tucked in closer to John and grasped his hand.

Together, John and Mary prayed for the Townsend family.

"Amen," John uttered with a bit of a sigh. Mary squeezed his hand.

"Let's go up to bed now, John. It has been a full day."

"I'll just settle this fire down. Then, I'll be up," John replied.

With full hearts, the Stuarts ended the day the way they began it, on their knees together and with God.

8

A Countryside Christmas

Christmas morning dawned white and bright. The week before, Jane had sent her package off to Father with a warm woollen scarf tucked inside. It was bright red and thick, and she felt so proud of her work. She imagined it wrapped round him on bitter, cold nights. Suddenly, Jane realized she heard singing. It was floating up the stairs. Mummy, who usually shared her room when she visited the farm, wasn't anywhere in their room. Jane sat quite still, listening. It was John and Mary, singing an English carol with great gusto:

God rest ye merry, gentlemen,
Let nothing you dismay,
For Jesus Christ our Saviour
Was born on Christmas Day,
To save us all from Satan's power
When we had gone astray.

   O tidings of comfort and joy,
   Comfort and joy;
   O tidings of comfort and joy!

She hurried to get dressed and down the stairs. There were sweets and treats laid out in the living room. A crackling fire was aflame. Mother and Henry were already downstairs. John and Mary were bustling about. Mary had rolls and marmalade, biscuits, and chocolate all laid out prettily on trays.

"What is the song you are singing?" she cried as she entered the room.

"Why, it is 'God Rest Ye Merry Gentlemen,'" Mary said. "Have you never heard of it?"

"I've never heard it so close to my ears," Jane replied with a twinkle in her eye. John and Mother laughed.

"It's a song that speaks to the joy we have in Jesus on this wonderful day. We have peace and joy and hope in Him, and nothing can take that away," Mary continued. "John and I just love this song. Jesus is the Good News of Peace and Comfort and Joy. Who doesn't need a bit of that this time of year with the war at hand?" She finished setting drinks out for everyone. "Happy Christmas! Oh, let's celebrate with joy at Orchard Glen Farm," she cried.

"Happy Christmas! Merry Christmas!" Mother, Jane, and Henry all chorused together.

They gathered round to exchange gifts. Mother pulled an envelope out from where she had hidden it in her pocket.

"I have a special gift for you, Jane and Henry. It is a letter from Father," she said.

Jane and Henry crowded round as Mother began to read aloud:

My dear darling Jane and strong soldier Henry,

I can't tell you how glad I am to know that you are celebrating Christmas with Mummy and the Stuarts at Orchard Glen Farm. I want you to know that I am quite safe and doing well. The Royal Air Force is just getting started, and more and more pilots are being trained and called up each day. Do your best at school for me and for Britain. Be good to Mummy and help the Stuarts. Make the most of your time there. Life in the English countryside is something special for sure. Always thinking of you and sending ever so many hugs and kisses across the miles.

All my love,

Daddy

Daddy's letter was postmarked from Canada. He was helping in the massive effort to train and recruit pilots under the British Commonwealth Air Training Plan. Canada was an ideal location, with its open fields and safe skies. It was just one of several locations where air force training was in full force as Britain and her allies prepared to face Germany.

Jane sighed when Mummy finished. How she

missed Daddy! She could almost hear his strong, kind voice as Mummy read the letter aloud. She leaned in closer. Henry stood up straight; his chest puffed out just a bit stronger. He would be a good soldier and make Daddy proud! Mummy had her own private letter from Daddy. What it said, Jane never knew, but she knew Mummy treasured it and kept it close to her heart.

Later that afternoon, Mummy was helping Mary in the kitchen. They were preparing potatoes and biscuits for that evening. Mary's golden hair was curling round her face, and Mummy's cheeks were red; her eyes were happy, but there was something serious behind their sparkle.

"Mary, have you always been so sure about Christ's love?" Helen asked quietly.

"Not always," Mary answered with a smile, "but I am now, and I am ever so grateful. Trusting in the Lord takes a step of faith—a belief, if you will. He speaks to us through His creation, through the scriptures, even through the great hymns that touch our hearts for Him. Often, He speaks to us through other people." With that, Mary looked Helen straight in the eye. "It is the dearest prayer of John and mine that you all would feel the great, true love of God here in this place and with us."

"I never really thought about God before the war," Helen said. "It sure does feel different here, though. Safe. Bright. Thank you, Mary. I think you and John are the most caring people I've ever met."

"Anytime you want to chat about any of this, just

let me know," Mary offered. "It's a blessing to have you here."

Henry and Jane were together upstairs in Jane's room. They were looking over Christmas gifts and making plans.

"Do you think God really loves us?" Henry asked suddenly. Jane looked at him.

"I'm not sure. We never knew much about God before we came to the farm. It sure is nice here. I think Uncle John and Aunt Mary really love God. It seems like He loves them, too. If He loves them, maybe He could love us?" Jane answered. Henry thought about this a bit.

"It sure would be nice to ask God to protect Daddy," he said quietly.

"I know," Jane said. "I'm just not sure if He would hear us."

At three o'clock that afternoon, everyone gathered together again to listen to the king's speech on the wireless. King George VI would address the nation, a tradition started by his father that he chose to carry on. Over the speakers, the king's voice crackled, encouraging Britain to remain undaunted and fight against darkness. He closed by saying,

> A new year is at hand. We cannot tell which it will bring. If it brings peace, how thankful we shall all be. If it brings continued struggle, we shall remain undaunted.
>
> In the meantime, I feel that we may all find a message of encouragement in the lines which, in my closing words, I would like to say to you.
>
> I said to the man who stood at the gate of the year, "Give me a light that I may tread safely into the unknown." And he replied, "Go out into the darkness and put your hand into the hand of God. That shall be to you better than light and safer than a known way.
>
> May that Almighty hand guide and uphold us all.[1]

---

1   King George VI. "Christmas Day Speech." December 25, 1939.

Jane listened and thought to herself, "How can I put my hand into the hand of God? Is He my light and safety?"

That night, tucked into bed on what had been a very happy Christmas Day despite the never-ending ache for Daddy, she lay still and thought deeply about everything in her heart. Snippets of songs floated through her mind. Fragments of Mary's prayers floated there, too. "What did it mean to love God? What did it mean if He loved her?" she thought. Then, in the quiet darkness, Jane uttered her very first small prayer, and it was just, "Help me, God." She didn't know it yet, but God heard, and even before she ever prayed, He was already at work.

9

Dunkirk Miracle

Late Spring 1940

Winston Churchill was chosen as the new Prime Minister (the head of the British government), and every night the news from the wireless was full of war developments. Safe at Orchard Glen Farm, Jane and Henry were free from any threat of bombs. Food rationing had begun, but happily, they didn't feel it whatsoever with Uncle John and Aunt Mary. It was starting to get harder and harder for Mummy, though. Uncle

John and Aunt Mary had begun to talk to her about relocating to the farm for the remainder of the war. One evening, news began to filter in about trouble around the English Channel. Germany was rapidly advancing through France, and the English army had gone to help the French fight. France and England were soundly defeated by Germany despite their best efforts. Desperate, the English army retreated, but they were now trapped on the edge of France. The British army was in danger of complete annihilation in France; the English Channel was the only way of escape. German fighter planes patrolled overhead, and the German army closed in. In the face of certain destruction, King George issued an astonishing proclamation over the wireless: he called for a National Day of Prayer to be held all over England on May 26, 1940. All of Britain was to rally and pray on behalf of the troops trapped at Dunkirk. Mary and John looked at each other. Without a doubt, they would join England in praying for God's intervention. Several days later,

Jane and Henry had a letter from Mummy. She would be attending a prayer meeting in London and urged them to pray hard for Daddy and for all the brave ones, for this battle involved them all—the air force, the navy, and the army.

The morning of Sunday, May 26, John hooked Chester and Ginger to the cart. They lifted their shining heads and snorted. Their feet pranced gently in place. John and Mary helped the children climb in. They were getting ready to head to the village church to gather with others to pray that God would protect the troops. Mummy was going to church in London, too. Everyone was united to ask God for safety on behalf of the lives of hundreds of men fighting against the destructive German army that was sweeping rapidly through the European nations. Everyone was going to pray that the troops could be rescued from Dunkirk. Pressed together with Henry in the cart, Jane gripped the side of the cart. Her belly was flip-flopping up and down. They were jolting down the road, but Jane was gazing straight ahead, not seeing anything. The terror of the thought that her daddy could be flying in enemy fire filled her mind, and she had to swallow back a scream that wanted to let loose from her lips. It wasn't like Jane to scream, but these days weren't like any days she had ever known either. Mary looked back over her shoulder.

"Are you alright, Jane, dear?" she asked with concern. Jane's gray eyes were wide, and her skin was stark white. She gulped. Henry looked over at her. His big blue eyes were too large in his small face. The unruly blond thatch was pressed neatly down on his head, thanks to Mary's strong comb.

"She's just stuck a bit, feelin' scared for Daddy," he offered, with a bit of a twang. He gave her a rough little pat. "It's alright, Jane. God will hear our prayers," he said firmly.

"We're almost there, Jane. I think you'll feel a bit better at the church," Mary said. Her brow wrinkled with concern. John's voice rose over the clip-clop of the horses.

"You just hold tight now, Jane. We're going to pray and see what the good Lord does on behalf of His people. I believe He's got us in the palm of His hand." John's words blew Jane's scream right away, and suddenly she was feeling much calmer. With a start, she realized John had been singing, and she had missed the first part of the song in her fear. He was now singing the second half of "God Moves in a Mysterious Way." John and Mary sang this hymn so often, it was becoming very familiar to the children:

Judge not the Lord by feeble sense,
But trust Him for His grace;
Behind a frowning providence,
He hides a smiling face.
His purposes will ripen fast,
Unfolding every hour;
The bud may have a bitter taste,
But sweet will be the flow'r.
Blind unbelief is sure to err
And scan His work in vain;
God is His own interpreter,

And He will make it plain.

Jane listened carefully and thought hard. It certainly was a grim circumstance right now. Trusting the Lord for His grace and resting in His goodness even when everything looked dark and scary was hard. How could she do that? The deep, gentle rumble of John's voice rolled over everyone in the cart. Henry gave her a tight squeeze, and Mary sighed a bit of relief. They rolled into the churchyard and found people everywhere. Horses and carts were hitched up outside, and more people were arriving on foot.

Jane saw Harriet and Tory at the church. Louie was over there, too, with his big brother, Ben. And there was Teacher, and why, the grocer, and the butcher, and . . . Jane sucked in a breath. Everyone in the entire village and outlying farms was here. The cool stone walls of the church closed around them gently. Dappled light shone through stained glass. The beauty and peace brought a holy stillness. People moved about with grave, respectful faces. The quiet was so thick Jane thought she could touch it if she tried. Here and there, people were kneeling to pray. The solemn, reverent Spirit rested upon everyone, and Jane felt her heart drawn toward a peculiar peace.

All of England was on her knees, beseeching God for a miracle.

Jane was kneeling next to Mary, feeling comforted by the solid faith flowing from her and the deep assurance felt in her prayers. She wanted that security, too. Inside her heart she whispered to the Lord, "Almighty Lord, be real to me. Help me to know You. Forgive me all my wrongs and help me to do right each day. Merciful Lord, here is my heart. It is Yours. Let me truly know Your love, and help me love You, too. Through Jesus Christ, I pray. Amen." In that moment a tingling anticipation and joy filled Jane. She was taking a step of faith. More than that, she knew—really knew—she was not alone anymore. She found herself fervently asking God for rescue and safety for Britain, for the army, the air force, the navy . . . for Daddy. She looked up and found her cheeks were wet with tears. Henry was next to her, his golden head solemnly bowed and his small hands clutched together tightly. She put her arm around him in a hug. He blinked and looked up at her.

"What is it?" he whispered. Jane just smiled. She would tell him later, and she would try to help him know God's love.

Later, Jane, Henry, Mary, and John learned much more about the important events that were put in motion that very day through the power of prayer. Over the wireless and through newspaper accounts, everyone realized how close they had been to total defeat. The Battle of Dunkirk had been an impossible one, but God had mysteriously stayed the enemy's hand. Somehow, the troops were miraculously evacuated—in part because of an unexplained halt on advancement, and in part because of the calmest, stillest waters the English Channel had seen in decades. Fog and clouds provided cover that hid men from the *Luftwaffe*[1] and allowed for the troops' miraculous escape. Local people on the English side of the channel worked together with the British forces, using every boat and vessel available to man, to evacuate the troops from the deadly beaches. All of Britain stood together in one united spirit. It was an answer to prayer, and all the newspapers and everyone everywhere called it a miracle.

The Battle of Dunkirk was the first real action Daddy would have faced, and Jane was scared. He had left the training grounds in Canada and had been stationed in battle. The Royal Air Force was patrolling to help secure the safe evacuation of hundreds of thousands of Allied Troops. The Royal Air Force was facing a direct attack by the *Luftwaffe*. There was a horrible time when Mummy, Jane, and Henry didn't know if Daddy was safe or not. But finally, they all had a letter. He had made it through. All was well.

---

1   German Air Force

My dear, dear Jane and Henry,

How glad I am to write this letter to you. I am well. I am safe. I can never tell you the courage of our soldiers, sailors, and pilots. How everyone rallied together to rescue the armed forces. It was something to behold. We were outnumbered, but somehow we succeeded. There are some who say that it was the National Day of Prayer that secured our miraculous escape. I have to say, I believe it. I really think God is on our side in this war. I know He is watching over me. There is a dark evil on the other side, and it seems to me that God is all that is Good and Light. Mummy has shared some with me about the Stuarts and their belief in the Lord. I want you to listen to them, children. Being up in the air with so little protecting me from death has made God so real to me. How happy I am to be able to write this letter to you! Well, that's all for now. I love you!

Be good to Mummy,
Your loving Daddy.

10

God Moves in a Mysterious Way

Summer 1940

A robin trilled, open throated, in the apple tree. Jane looked up from where she was reading and smiled.

"Small mite with such heart," she mused. The sunshine fell in golden waves and shone on her dark hair. A blue sky just like a robin's egg stretched overhead, and puffy cotton ball clouds dotted the sky. Jane often retreated to the orchards on the farm, especially now that it was summer and school had let out. The quiet and beauty and sense of living, growing things brought her peace and calm. She could hardly remember life in London, and sometimes that worried her. What would happen when it was time to go back? The truth was, there was no real way to know how long this war was going to stretch on. In a sense, she knew it was just beginning. How grateful she was that Mummy and Dad had decided to have her and Henry stay put. So many children had been evacuated and returned to London, only to re-evacuate and then move around. Instead, she and Henry had built another life in the English countryside, and somehow she felt so secure. Uncle John and Aunt Mary loved them all like family; she knew that for sure.

Jane mulled thoughts over in her mind, laying her book aside. Prime Minister Churchill had recently declared that the Battle of Britain was about to begin. She shivered. The Battle of Britain meant that Hitler and Germany were coming against England to conquer all. She felt a bubble of fear rise up in her belly. She pushed it aside and squinched her eyes shut tightly. Inside she prayed, "God, protect Daddy. Help Britain. Help me to be brave."

"Jane! Jane, where are you?" It was Henry. Jane sat up. His voice sounded wrong.

"I'm here, Henry!" she answered. She was already standing up, tucking her book under her arm and beginning to move toward his voice.

"Mummy is here. You must come right away to the house." Jane felt that scared feeling rising up again. What was Mummy doing here during the week? Something wasn't right. The children started to run together toward the house. Jane said nothing at all. She didn't ask any questions, and Henry didn't offer anything. Together, they rushed.

They skidded to a stop at the kitchen door and slowly went in. Mummy was standing in the kitchen with Aunt Mary. She turned to look at the children. Aunt Mary turned, too, and stood strong right next to Mother.

"Daddy's been wounded," she began and stopped.

Her eyes brimmed with tears, and her lip trembled. She took a big breath. "I must go to him. I had the telegram yesterday evening. I took the first possible train. The Battle of Britain has truly begun . . ." She stopped suddenly and lowered her face to hide the struggle from the children. Mary put her arm around Mummy's shoulder. She looked at Jane and Henry. Her blue eyes were grave, and the blond curls framed her face in slight disarray.

"Your mum's strong and brave. You children will stay right here with Uncle John and me. We are going to trust God for your father's life just as we have been doing all these days so far." Jane started to cry. Henry stared hard at the floor. "It's okay, loves. It's okay," Mary murmured. Mummy came close and pulled the children to her. Jane felt Mummy's strength and her love and her sorrow. With a gulp, Jane swallowed back a sob. She couldn't think straight, and she didn't know what to say.

"I have to leave first thing in the morning, darlings. It is a long journey to get to Father, and

I must go right away. I had to come to tell you in person. I couldn't imagine you reading this news in a letter and not getting a chance to hug you and look at your faces."

"Oh, Mummy," Jane whispered. How dear, how deeply dear Mummy was to her.

"Let's get you a bite to eat," Mary said. "We've all had such a shock." She bustled around the kitchen, setting out a quick tea for everyone. Nourishing food had a settling effect and a way of setting the body to rights. Jane and Henry struggled to eat but found it did indeed help them feel a bit more settled. Mummy sipped the nourishing tea, made from Mary's own raspberry plants, stirred with honey, and nibbled a biscuit. The warm milk and hot tea warmed them from the inside out, bringing a soothing feeling to them all.

"It's funny how a shock can make you cold," Jane thought. It was midsummer, but the drinks were just right.

Uncle John was to take Mummy in the morning.

God Moves in a Mysterious Way

Jane and Henry were welcome to come, too, to see her off. The Stuarts worked hard to be a steady source of God's light and love to the family that evening; in truth, they were rattled, too, because the Townsends had all grown so dear to them. They felt like they knew Daddy personally, although they had not yet met him in person.

Before bed, Mummy sat on the edge of Jane's bed with Henry tucked under her arm. Jane was settled with the covers pulled right up under her chin, as if somehow the blankets could shield her from all fear.

"I'm trying to trust God, Mummy," Jane said quietly. Mummy squeezed her hand.

"We've learned a lot about God's love here at Orchard Glen Farm, and we've felt His love through the Stuarts. I am glad you are trying to trust God," Mummy said.

"I prayed to know God in my heart," Jane said after a bit. Henry looked at her with big eyes.

Mummy replied, "Daddy and I have been writing

letters back and forth about this very thing. You know, it's interesting the way we both seemed to be hearing the same message from different places all at the same time." She nestled in a bit closer to the children.

"God moves in a mysterious way," Jane said. "Uncle John and Aunt Mary sing a song with those words all the time. I think it's really true."

"I'm scared," Henry said in a small voice.

"Oh darling, I'm scared, too," Mummy said. She squeezed each of their hands with a loving grip. "You have both been so brave and good. Look how you've learned to help around the farm with the Stuarts. You both handle so much work around the farm, and you know, I think you are really a blessing to John and Mary. I am so proud of you. You have been strong for Britain and strong for Mummy and Dad. Let's ask God to help us know His love, and maybe we can ask Him to help us be brave through Him. He can give us the power to do what is right and to be a light during these dark days."

"Henry, remember these words." Jane began to sing a bit of "God Moves in a Mysterious Way," the hymn so often sung to them.

Ye fearful saints, fresh courage take;
The clouds ye so much dread,
Are big with mercy and shall break,
In blessings on your head.

"I think this means we can look to God to help us find His goodness even in the hard times, even with Daddy injured, even with this dreadful war. He can make us brave," Mummy said. "Let us say a prayer." Mummy and Henry bowed their heads, and Jane closed her eyes. She couldn't believe Mummy was praying. Despite her fear and sadness for Daddy, light and joy were rising in her heart. Mummy and God! Deep delight shot through her from head to toe.

Jane lay quietly, alone after Mummy had left to settle Henry and take a few moments with John and Mary before bed. Aunt Mary had placed clusters of summer roses throughout the house. The scent was floating in the air. The beauty reminded her of God's love. She breathed deeply; tomorrow would soon be at hand.

11

Goodbye for Now

Jane and Henry stood with Mummy and Uncle John on the platform. Jane felt a strange, familiar feeling. Mummy had her satchel under her arm, and she was smartly dressed in a dark suit with a small matching hat pinned to her head.

The train was coming into the station; the sound of the whistle rang in the air. With a whoosh, the train jolted to a stop.

"It's time for me to be off," Mummy said quietly.

Jane and Henry stood tall next to her; they were both bound and determined to be brave.

"Goodbye, Mummy! Give Daddy our love. Write to us as soon as you can." Jane squeezed Mummy's hand and then hugged her hard. Mummy pulled her close. The dark head pressed against her suit jacket, the dear freckled face held close.

"Oh Jane, I love you so. How proud I am of how you've helped Henry these days. I will be sure to tell everything to Daddy, and especially about God's love."

"Goodbye, Mummy," Henry said carefully. "I will write to you with Jane's help."

"My dear boy," Mummy choked a bit and then managed to go on, "I will write as soon as I can and give your love and prayers to Daddy." Henry nodded, his golden head shining in the morning light.

John held out his hand to Helen. "Blessings on your travel. We'll be praying for William every day and for you. Don't you worry for a minute about

Jane and Henry. We love 'em like our own. You'll always have a place with us." Mummy clasped his hand, her eyes brimming and then, with determination, she grabbed her satchel and turned to board the train.

This time it was Jane and Henry who stood on the platform trying to bravely smile as Mummy waved from the window. This time it was Jane and Henry who watched the train launch off and push away into the distance, becoming smaller and smaller and smaller. The curl of smoke vanished into the sky with a suddenness that felt final. An empty feeling seemed to sweep over the children, and they drooped just a bit, just a wee bit. John noticed it right away.

"Come now," he said gravely. "Let's load up and get back to Orchard Glen Farm. I heard Aunt Mary say she had a peach pie she was working on getting ready to go into the oven. Perhaps it'll be all ready for us by the time we get back." The children turned, and hand in hand, walked with John to

Ginger and Chester. Faithful Ginger and Chester, the ones who had brought them to Orchard Glen Farm on a day that felt so long ago. The ones who swept apples off the palms of their hands and let them brush and curry them until they shone. All the memories of Orchard Glen Farm filled Jane's mind. The rose garden and the apple trees. Her own dear room. The kitchen work and the henhouse. Somehow, she knew it was going to be okay. No matter what, she knew they had Uncle John and Aunt Mary to help them wait for Mummy and Dad. No matter what, they also had God, and He did move in a mysterious way. Jane was coming to realize that His way was good, even when she didn't understand and even when it sometimes hurt. The sunshine was golden and bright as they headed back to the farm. It was bright like hope, like a safe future, like victory, like love—God's love that wrapped round them every day at Orchard Glen Farm. Uncle John didn't say much, but he did sing. Jane looked at Henry and smiled. The song rumbled around and over them, and Jane found she was beginning to understand.

That night, Jane lay in her bed looking up at the ceiling. She was thinking hard. The future was still uncertain. Her gas mask lay ever present on the table nearby, though there had been no need to use it yet. The Battle of Britain had just begun. Father was injured, and Mummy was gone away to help him. Yet, somehow, she knew with a sureness that took her breath away; she knew that she was not alone. No matter what the future held, God's love was dawning in her heart, and the day would last forever. Lines from Uncle John's song "God Moves in a Mysterious Way" floated up from her heart to her mind:

His purposes will ripen fast,
Unfolding every hour;
The bud may have a bitter taste,
But sweet will be the flow'r.

Could she trust in the God she was coming to so dearly know? Could He truly bring something sweet out of what felt so bitter in this moment? Jane took a deep breath. With God's help, she knew she could trust Him.

It was the time of the Second World War.

For Jane and for Henry, Britain's Operation Pied Piper, the great evacuation of hundreds of thousands of children, was more than a holiday; it was more than an adventure; it was a divine encounter that connected their lives with Mary and John, sheltered at Orchard Glen Farm.

JANE AND HENRY:

A WORLD WAR II ADVENTURE

A Sequel

Table of Contents

1. Letters for Jane. 110
2. News for Orchard Glen Farm. 118
3. Special Arrival. 128
4. How Sweet the Name of Jesus Sounds. 135
5. Peace Which Passeth All Understanding. 151
6. Letters from London. 162
7. Aunt Mary Goes to Town. 170
8. The Women's Institute. 178
9. Be Anxious for Nothing. 182
10. Christmas Surprise. 193
11. The Lord Is My Light and My Salvation, Whom Shall I Fear?. 206
12. The Notice. 215
13. God Moves in a Mysterious Way, His Wonders to Perform. 223
14. Orchard Glen Farm Forever. 231

Appendix. 238

1

Letters for Jane

Late Summer 1940

Jane clutched the letter in her hand, staring absently at the clear blue sky above her. Her other hand gripped the stiff grass at her side with a tight fist. Jane was slight, with dark hair falling over her shoulders in two tight braids. Her gray eyes peered pensively out of a creamy, slightly freckled face. English countryside undulated green and gold, rising gently around her; Orchard Glen Farm, the home where she and her small brother, Henry, were billeted,[1] was just over the slight hill.

It was hard to believe they had been at Orchard Glen Farm for almost a year. Part of Britain's Operation Pied Piper, she and Henry had been moved from London to the safety of the English countryside in the fall of 1939, far from any terror or harm from the war. They had been lovingly chosen when they arrived in the countryside by the Stuarts, now known as Uncle John and Aunt Mary, and had been safely nestled at Orchard Glen Farm ever since.

She could hear the low of a cow, carried on the slight breeze, and the sounds of birdsong filled the air. Jane breathed deeply; the air was pungent and warm and mingled around her, adding to the pristine beauty. Sweet daisies and white clover grew abundantly, spangling the green pasture and meadow like a handful of stars scattered to wink and glow among the hillsides. The comforting sights and sounds did little to break through the anxiety

---

1   Lodged at a countryside farmhouse due to the war.

that was trying to gain control of her heart and thoughts.

The letter crumpled in her hand was from Mother, and it brought news to the farm about Father.

Almost two months ago Father, a Royal Air Force pilot, had been wounded in the Battle of Dunkirk, and Mother had hurried off to the War Hospital to be at his side. Jane and Henry had been left in the care of Uncle John and Aunt Mary, just as they had been since first evacuated last fall. The days since Mother had boarded the train, swooshing off in a puff of smoke and steam, had been an agony of hope and worry for Jane.

Mother sent regular letters from the hospital, updating everyone at Orchard Glen Farm on Father's progress. Full of joy and newfound faith, Mother shared the good and just a tidbit of the bad, too. Father had a bit of a rough time at first with fever, and then there was a scare of serious infection. He pulled through, however, and was continuing to mend. Jane was comforted by Mother's letters: they were newsy, lighthearted, full of details about Father and hope for the future. She always felt peace and a bit of happiness when reading the letters. Sometimes, she would read them again and again, just to hear Mother's voice in her head.

Aunt Mary and Uncle John were a comfort, too. They were helping Jane understand how to trust God through this scary time and praying with her and Henry for their Father's speedy healing. Jane was learning how to be brave and strong. Trusting God was new to Jane, but the knowledge of a great, wholehearted love was dawning in her heart and mind. Every week that went by found her growing more deeply in her understanding of this great love.

But now this.

The letter clutched fiercely in her hand was going to require yet more from her. She squeezed her eyes shut tight and pressed her lips together. Taking a deep breath, she smoothed out the crumpled letter and read it again.

Dear Mary, John, sweet Jane, and darling Henry,

Greetings from Father's bedside! I am writing swiftly today as there is a busy hustle of preparations at the hospital. The nurses have been in and out tending to this and that. Father sends his great love to you all. I am happy to say that every day he grows stronger.

I hope all is well on the farm. Jane and Henry, I trust you are doing your best by Uncle John and Aunt Mary. How many eggs have you brought in each day from the chickens, Henry? How is the garden, Jane?

I have real news to share with you all today. The physician has visited and pronounced Father well. His injury has almost fully mended, and he has been deemed fit to return to service. A few weeks from now, he will depart the hospital and rejoin the Royal Air Force. I will return to London and continue war efforts from there. I plan to stay at our London home as long as possible. In other even happier news, I hope to be able to visit you all at the farm in September.

 I know the relief over Father's recovery is clouded by the thought of him flying into such extreme danger again. We must be brave for Father, dears. We must be brave for England and do our part. John and Mary, all my love and gratitude to you. Henry, chin up and take courage. Jane, look to God and keep an eye out for Henry, always.

 Forever grateful for Orchard Glen Farm and our Merciful Lords great love,

Yours,
Helen (Mummy)

Tucked inside this letter was a folded piece of paper with just Jane's name on it. This was a private note just for Jane from Mummy with a bit of Father's handwriting scrawled on it, too. Jane swiped at tears with the back of her hand. This little bit of paper read:

Jane dear,

A little note just for you to tell you to be of good courage. I know these are trying times and fearful, too. So proud of you, Jane, for how you help Aunt Mary and look out for Henry. Carry on in this good work. I will see you soon.

You have all my love and prayers,

Mummy

Father's words scrawled across the bottom of the page:

Darling Jane,

How proud I am of you. Keep strong, my girl. I know it must be frightening to think of me in the skies again after my injury, but I know God is with me, and He is in control. I sense Him near me, and I know He is teaching all of us more about who He is. We have learned so much of His love from the Stuarts. Let's continue to trust in His merciful kindness. Surely it is always right to fight against the wrong. The battle is needed, and the fight is for good. Remember that, dear, when you are scared. Think of me in the skies. God be with you and me until we meet again.

Your loving Daddy

Jane took in a shuddering breath. Blinking away tears, the blue sky came into vivid focus. Suddenly all the sounds around her seemed loud and near. She looked up at a sky that arched over her head like a great dome. So peaceful, it seemed impossible to think of anything harsh, ugly, or scary marring the great open expanse of blue goodness. In her heart, she whispered a tiny prayer: "Merciful Lord, protect Father. Be with us in this great battle. Let the victory be won for England. Help me to be strong, O Heavenly Father. I trust in You. Through Jesus Christ, I pray, Amen."

2

News for Orchard Glen Farm

Mary sloshed the water in the bucket vigorously with the mop. She pushed a strand of golden hair off her face with the back of her wrist and straightened her shoulders. Time in the meadow would do Jane good. It always did. Her heart throbbed a bit. How she loved these wee ones who had come to her and John from London. Brave mites. Mary put some water down onto the flagstone floor and began scrubbing with the mop.

The door pushed open with a boyish bang, and Henry appeared with a basket full of eggs and a big smile stretched across his face. His thatch of gold hair stood up in a shock all over his head.

"Hullo, there!" Mary said, straightening up again and answering with a matching grin.

"We've got a dozen eggs today, Aunt Mary."

"Well, I am glad," she answered with a relieved sigh. Food rationing, a big part of the war effort, was starting to really affect everyone in England, even the farmers. "Go on over and carefully wash them for me." She nodded in the direction of the wash basin and water supply. Henry had been washing eggs for a while and had learned to be careful and thorough. He headed over to the wash station.

The door pushed open again and John entered. Mary looked up at him and noticed his brow was furrowed and he looked a bit tense.

"John!" she cried out happily. "I wasn't expectin' to see you so soon. It's not near teatime." She smiled at her husband.

"Hullo, Uncle John!" Henry called from across the kitchen. John's face eased into a smile as he saw them both, relaxing a little with the pleasure of their greeting.

"I have some news, Mary. I wanted to come in right away to share it. Where's Jane? Is she nearby? I'd like to tell everyone at once, and I didn't want to wait 'til this evening. I might be late for tea, anyhow."

Mary dropped her mop gently and wiped her hands on her apron. "She's just out in the meadow. I gave her some time with the letter from her Mum and Dad. Let me see where she's at." She moved over to the door and opened it. Jane was coming across the pasture to the farm. Mary waved and smiled at her. "Come on in, Jane!" she called. "Uncle John has some news for us."

Jane started to hurry faster, and soon she was running. She arrived at the door just a bit out of breath, with a rosy flush in her cheeks and a bright twinkle in her eyes—the countryside's wholesome air and vigor had indeed done her good. Mary gently ushered her into the kitchen. Henry had come close once more, and the two children pressed near to Mary while they looked at Uncle John with big eyes. He smiled at the threesome, so dear to his heart. Mary was standing strong just behind the children as if the strength in her frame would support them all, no matter what may come.

"I've had some news that I want to share wi' you all right away," he began carefully. "First, more children are being evacuated from London and other cities around England. We've been asked if we can take on one more." He stopped for a moment and looked at Mary and the children, giving them a moment to take it in. "And second, today I had another visit from the War Ag.[1] Farmers are being asked to increase production and increase their farmlands. We are going to have to plow and prepare additional fields on the farm. We'll all have to work together during harvest, and the start of

---

1   British War Agricultural Committee

school has been delayed." He paused, considering the faces before him.

John and Mary knew the war was having a huge impact on the British economy. In a fierce effort to survive and press forward to victory, Britain was calling upon farmers to produce more than ever before to try to compensate for the imported goods that were no longer available to the country due to battle. John learned just days ago that the War Ag would be monitoring Orchard Glen Farm, and all the other farms all over the country, to be sure the farms were producing enough and maximizing their output. Not only that, but with the start of the Battle of Britain,[2] the cities were experiencing severe danger. Now, more children were being evacuated, and children who had returned home earlier in the year were being sent out to the countryside once more. Jane and Henry had stayed put at Orchard Glen Farm, but that hadn't been the case for many children. It was time to welcome

---

[2] See *Jane and Henry: A World War II Adventure*

many back into safer living spaces. Nobody really knew how difficult it might actually get in the weeks and months to come.

"Oh, John," Mary said quietly. Her eyes sparkled with unshed tears. "Of course, we'll take another child. We'll all do our best to help you in the field." She spoke with confident firmness and placed a hand on each child's shoulder. Jane and Henry didn't say anything for a moment. Their minds whirled. Flexibility was key during wartime, and Jane and Henry were learning that every single day. Anything could change at any time.

One thing, though, would never change, and that was God's love, and Mummy and Dad's, and Aunt Mary and Uncle John's. They both knew it deep down inside now. They knew it was true.

"When will the new evacuees come?" Jane asked in a small voice. She had been so looking forward to the start of school. She swallowed back the lump. It would be fun to be out in the field with Uncle John. She knew that. She just had a lot to think about:

Father going up into the skies again, a late start with school, new fields on the farm, evacuees. Her mind spun a little.

John's eyes met Mary's across the room. She smiled just for him. John and Mary had talked about this together privately. They had room for more at Orchard Glen Farm. They both wanted to keep space for Jane and Henry's parents, with so much uncertainty in London and in the skies. Both John and Mary had opened their hearts to the Townsends and wanted them to know they were welcome in their home. But, even so, they could take on another child. Mary felt a shiver of joy thrill her. She couldn't help but wonder who this dear child would be.

"The new evacuees should be arriving in a day or so," John answered gravely. "I know there are a lot of changes for you, for us all. We'll get through it step by step. We can trust our loving Heavenly Father to guide us and sustain us."

Henry squirmed a bit next to Mary. "I'll help,

Uncle John." He spoke bravely and looked straight at the tall, strong man filling the space in the kitchen.

John smiled. "Don't I know it!" He spoke assurance to the young boy. Henry stood a little taller. Jane stood taller, too.

"What can we do now?" Jane asked.

"Well, I mus' be heading back out to the fields. Henry, would you like to come along with me? I am going to walk the land where we will put down some new fields. Mary, could you look to getting the space ready for our new evacuee? Jane, you could help Aunt Mary or come out to the fields with me." Henry was already across the room, sliding his hand into Uncle John's. Mary smiled again.

"I think I'll stay with Aunt Mary for now," Jane said. She felt a burden on her heart, and she knew Aunt Mary would be able to help.

"All right then, I'll see you later. I'll be back with this young man at least for teatime, if not myself." John and Henry headed out together across the yard.

"Jane, let's finish washing the eggs Henry was working on, and then we'll head up to the bedrooms to see what we can do for our new guest." Mary was moving her mop away and getting ready to swiftly finish the flagstone floor.

Jane went over to the eggs to get them finished up. Her mind swirled as she gently scrubbed. *Where would the new evacuee sleep? Would he or she be older or younger? Would the new evacuee come from London, too?*

3

Special Arrival

Jane was upstairs sweeping a broom vigorously over the floors when Aunt Mary appeared in the doorway.

"All right then, Jane. Let's see where we can put a new evacuee." Aunt Mary looked around the room. "Uncle John's been working on a simple bed frame in the barn. If we get a girl, we'll set her up in here; if a boy, we'll make way in Henry's room." An empty space on the opposite wall looked promising. Aunt Mary walked over and eyed up the measurements. "Let's move this small table over by the window," she said and quickly relocated it. Jane stepped in and swept the broom briskly over the area. Aunt Mary watched her for a moment. Jane was furiously sweeping and had a frown between her eyes. Aunt Mary placed a gentle hand on Jane's shoulder.

"Is everything all right, dear?" she asked. Jane's face crumpled, and she gulped back a cry. Aunt Mary gently led her to the bedside and sat down next to her. "Now, tell me what's the matter," she coaxed. Jane gulped again. The words were stuck in the back of her throat. Aunt Mary sat quietly next to her, with her hand on top of Jane's. Jane couldn't speak at all. Not a word would come out of her mouth. She thought if she let even one word out, everything would come tumbling out and she would never stop. She held everything in tight.

Quietly, Aunt Mary began to pray. Jane leaned her head against Aunt Mary's shoulder. Prayer and

Aunt Mary seemed to go together like two peas in a pod. She couldn't imagine one without the other. As Aunt Mary finished, Jane took in a deep, shuddering breath. She lifted her tear-stained face to Aunt Mary's. Mary smiled and smoothed her dark hair. Jane opened her mouth and then snapped it shut. A loud "Hullo!" echoed up the stairs from down in the kitchen. Jane and Aunt Mary looked at each other with wide eyes. *Who could that be?* They both stood up and, straightening apron and skirt and with one more quick swipe across the face to brush the tears away, they headed down the stairs.

Mr. Jones, the billeting officer, was standing in the kitchen with a small girl next to him. Not more than five or six, her honey-brown hair fell over her shoulders in disarray, and eyes like the spring sky glittered with unshed tears. Jane forgot herself and her troubles immediately as her heart went out to the troubled little girl. She knelt down in front of the little girl and smiled up into her small face.

"This 'ere's Anne," Mr. Jones began. "She's just

Special Arrival

come from the station and 'ad a right long journey. I brought her right over as soon as could be. John said you were willing to take in another. Goodness knows this one needs a home."

Mary shook off her great surprise. "Why, yes, Mr. Jones! We're so glad to have her. Hullo, Anne," she said, turning to the bewildered little girl with tenderness. "We're mighty glad to have you."

Small Anne just looked.

"Jane, why don't you take Anne out to the lav in the back. She's had a long journey," Mary advised astutely.

Jane stood up and took the little girl by the hand. Together, they went out the back to the garden path to the outhouse, now so familiar to Jane and kept pristinely clean by Mary.

"Thank you, Mary. We've had a load of evacuees come in. Seems like maybe fifteen children have come to this area just today alone to be placed into homes. Appreciate your efforts," Mr. Jones touched his cap in tribute to Mary.

"We're blessed to help. Thank you for bringing her. We weren't quite sure when to expect our next visitor."

"Things are starting to get a little hot in London and some of the other towns," Mr. Jones offered in a low voice. "People are coming to the countryside in droves. We'll do our part, that's for certain." He tipped his hand to his hat again. "Well, I'll be off now if you're sure you can get her settled?"

"Everything's fine here, Mr. Jones. I've got bedding and blankets at hand. We've room for Anne, and we welcome her to Orchard Glen Farm.

Special Arrival

John will sure be surprised! You saved us the trip in to bring her back. Thank you! There's so much work on the farm just now; it seems there is something at hand every minute." Mary saw Mr. Jones out the door. He had arrived in one of the first motorcars their small village had ever seen. He climbed in and was off in a puff of exhaust. Mary watched the car rattle down the country road in wonder. She thought about Anne. Surely a motorcar ride was a new experience for the child. So much newness in one day: trains, buses, cars, and now a home at Orchard Glen Farm.

Jane came back in with the little girl, who was looking a bit more relieved. Mary smiled to see the relief in her face.

"Anne's six," Jane said with a lilt in her voice. "She traveled all the way from London just like Henry and I."

"All by myself," Anne said in a small voice. "Teacher came so far as the station and then had to stay on to the next stop."

"Ah, I see," said Mary. "Well, you're not alone now," she offered kindly. "You're here with us, at Orchard Glen Farm. Please call me Aunt Mary. My husband John would be honored if you called him Uncle John. We're mighty glad to have you. Let's get you fed a bit and cleaned up. If you're up to it, we'll send a note right back to your Mum and Dad." Mary eyed the tag pinned to the little girl's coat.

In the next minute, she was busy putting out a jug of milk and some bread with a bit of jam for the small girl. Jane moved to show her how to wash to eat. They all sat down together at the table. Jane felt a small tug at her heart. She knew Anne would be her special charge, just like Henry, but in a different way, too. Anne needed a friend.

4

How Sweet the Name of Jesus Sounds

Jane took Anne out to Aunt Mary's garden and the orchard. Anne's big sky blue eyes were taking everything in at once. Aunt Mary's flowers were a riot of color and fragrance. The apples were swelling in the orchard.

"You'll like it here, Anne. Uncle John and Aunt Mary are wonderful. I can't wait for you to meet my brother, Henry. He's nine." Jane looked down at Anne, walking carefully next to her. Clearly, Anne wasn't quite ready to run and skip and barrel over hill and field. Jane knew she probably felt shocked inside and a little scared. She squeezed her hand reassuringly. Anne didn't say anything for a bit. She just looked. Jane thought perhaps she would like to see the farm animals. "Let's head over to the barn. You can see the chickens and Chester and Ginger, Uncle John's horses." Anne seemed to perk up just a bit with interest, and Jane led the way over to the barn.

The russet-colored barn welcomed them with the sounds of life and bustle. Chickens were scratching about; pigs grunted; a horse shook and stomped a foot; the quack of ducks carried in the breeze. The good, clean smell of fresh hay filled the air. Uncle John and Henry were walking the farm, surveying pasture and fields for new planting sites, so Chester and Ginger were out grazing in the adjoining pasture. Jane helped Anne climb up on the lowest rung of the fence so she could gaze out at the horses.

Suddenly, Anne spoke. "Which one's which?" Her voice was almost a whisper.

Jane smiled and pointed: "That's Chester, and over there—that's Ginger." Jane let out a whistle and grabbed a handful of thick, long grass. She helped Anne down off the fence and gave her a fistful of grass to hold in her hand. She showed Anne how to hold the grass flat in the palm of her hand. "Come on, Chester!" she called out to the shining brown horse. Chester came trotting over and pressed his soft nose right into Jane's face. Jane laughed. Anne looked a little scared. She had never been this close to such a big creature before.

"He wants some grass, Anne," she said and laughed again with joy. She held her hand out with the grass laid out flat across her palm. Chester's soft lips tickled her hand as she held the grass carefully; he gobbled it right up. "Your turn, Anne. Don't be scared. His mouth tickles," Jane encouraged, and Anne stretched her small hand bravely forward. Chester gently nuzzled the grass out of her hand, too. "You can pet him gently," Jane said and showed Anne how to stroke the horse's muzzle. Anne gave a little sigh, and something tight that had been bunched up in her little body seemed to ease right out. She took a deep breath, and her little frozen face relaxed into a smile.

"Thank you, Jane," she said carefully, blinking back tears and fighting a tremble in her lips.

"Let's go back in and see if we can help Aunt Mary get ready for teatime; it will soon be time

to eat. Maybe Henry will be back from the fields. Won't he be excited to meet you!" Jane exclaimed and turned Anne back toward the house, stepping quickly through the grass.

Inside, Mary had a big soup pot bubbling on her new gas cooker. New improvements were often coming their way these days, especially with so many on the home front needing to help the war effort. Anything that could make the housework just a bit easier and less time-consuming was high priority. The gas cooker was just one of these improvements. Mary was thrilled; cooking was easier, cleaner, and more efficient. A propane flame flickered at the bottom of the stove; the good smell of potatoes and bacon filled the kitchen from the steaming soup energetically bubbling on the hot plate. She had a loaf of bread tucked behind one of the doors to a heated compartment, keeping warm. She put a long wooden spoon into the soup and stirred carefully. Just then, she heard the kitchen door open and turned to see Jane and Anne.

"Hullo, there!" she called warmly.

"Hullo, Aunt Mary, we're here to wash up and see about helping you set the table," Jane answered.

"How did you get on, Anne?" she asked as the girls went to wash.

Anne looked over at her carefully. "Jane showed me the chickens, and Chester and Ginger," she said. Mary could tell from the sound of her voice that she had really enjoyed meeting the farm animals.

"Well, that's just fine. I bet Henry will enjoy some help with the chickens. Perhaps you can learn to put the feed down for them. We'll see about it with Uncle John later." The sound of heavy boots stomping off dirt was heard just outside the door, and Henry's excited voice rang out over the lower rumble of Uncle John's. "Why, John's back," Mary cried happily and hurried over to the entrance way. "John, Henry, our special visitor has arrived," she announced eagerly as they came in to head to the wash station. John stopped suddenly, and Mary smiled. "Meet Anne," she said warmly and gently brought the little girl forward. Shyly, Anne looked up at him.

"Well, now," Uncle John rumbled. "Welcome, welcome." He stuck out his hand for a shake and then realized it was quite dirty. With a grimace, he pulled it back. Everyone laughed. "Just one moment, while I wash up," he said with a chuckle. "So glad to have you here, Anne." He looked over the children's heads to Mary; she gave a slight nod. All was well at Orchard Glen Farm.

"Hi!" Henry greeted Anne loudly. "I'm Henry." His cheeks were rosy, and he had the fresh, windblown look that comes from an afternoon in the outdoors.

"Pleased to meet you, Henry," Anne answered shyly, trying to remember all her manners.

"We'll get the table set while you wash up. Are you able to sit down with us, John?" Mary was moving about helping Jane set out plates and soup bowls and preparing the table.

"I surely will sit down tonight, Mary. I don't want to miss the first time round the table with our new visitor," John answered. He would leave the work for just a little; it would still be there tomorrow. He could head out to tend to some work around the house right after tea.

Mary lit the candles. Soon, it would be time to put the blackout boards into the windows. All of England remained under a mandatory blackout and each night had to seal up and shield every little crack or crevice that light could escape from. Even out here, in the deep English countryside, if even a glimmer of light was seen, a hefty fine was given. Blacking out all the light protected the people; the German bombers couldn't figure out where to let loose their bombs without any light to guide or direct them. Aunt Mary looked at the clock. The summer evening hours were still keeping sunlight late. There would be time to tuck the house into blackout after the meal.

The table was set and the candles flickered

warm and bright in brass candleholders on the red-checked tablecloth. A sweet-smelling vase full of Mary's wonderful rich red and white roses glimmered in the dancing light. Mary spooned the fragrant soup into bowls and placed big chunks of bread in the center of the table.

"Sit here, Anne," Aunt Mary invited, pulling out a chair for her and warmly pressing her forward. Anne took her seat gratefully. It had been a long day.

Once everyone was seated, Uncle John grabbed hold of Mary and Henry's hands and everyone followed suit. Henry grabbed Jane's and Jane grabbed Anne's. To Anne's surprise, she found her hands gently held by Aunt Mary and Jane.

Uncle John bent his head to pray. Anne looked around the table and saw everyone else bow their heads, too. Quickly, she ducked her head down and squinched her eyes shut tight. As he began to speak, Anne cast a sidelong look at Jane and Henry. Their eyes were shut tight, and they seemed to be listening hard. She closed her eyes again. As soon as

Uncle John said "Amen," Jane and Henry grabbed up their spoons. Anne grabbed hers, too. Carefully, she dipped her spoon into the steaming bowl, trying not to drip.

Mary looked across the table at John. "John, I forgot. We don't yet have the bed set up for Anne in Jane's room. The bed frame is out there in the barn, ready to go, and I've got the quilts all stitched and filled. When do you think you'll be able to get it set up? Dear Anne looks completely done in." John and Mary glanced together at the little girl. She could hardly keep her eyes open as she tried to eat her soup and bread. John pushed his chair back from the table.

"I'll just tend to this right now. Let Anne finish and get washed up. Her bed will be ready in no time." He was already striding out the door before the words had finished coming from his mouth. Mary smiled after him, a bit surprised. She hadn't expected him to get up immediately to take care of Anne's need; she had already been planning ways to squeeze Jane and Anne into the one bed in the room, just for the night, if needed. Everyone had worked long and hard that day, especially John, who was manfully trying to convert the farm into the production level required by the War Ag. Her heart filled with love; John truly cared about others' comforts and needs. Strong and steady as a rock, he willingly put others' needs before his own.

"That was kind of Uncle John," Henry said, his mouth full of potato and bread.

"Don't talk with food in your mouth, Henry," Mary admonished gently. "Yes, it was kind. Uncle John is a good man." Henry ducked his head bashfully and swallowed down his food in a gulp.

"The Lord's been kind to give me Uncle John and Daddy," he said quickly.

Jane looked over at him, surprised at his faith-filled words. He looked rosy and strong, confident in his young, boyish ways. She smiled and happiness bloomed all over her creamy face, and light filled her sea-gray eyes. "The Lord's been good to all of us at Orchard Glen Farm. Thank you, Aunt Mary," she said simply.

Mary flushed a little. She didn't expect such gratitude from the children. What a delight they were. "What a blessing you all are!" she said, suddenly. She couldn't help it. "It fills Uncle John and me with such joy to have you here with us."

Anne looked on with wide eyes, stunned out of her sleepiness. She was experiencing what Jane and Henry had when they first arrived at the farm: love, prayers, and lots of talk about God. It was all new to her, and she wasn't quite sure what to make of it. She had never been called a blessing before. She blinked. Jane looked over at her knowingly. She could just imagine how bewildered the little girl felt. She determined to help this new friend adjust to her new place and show her God's love.

"Let's finish up eating," Mary interrupted Jane's reverie. "I want to help Anne get all washed up and settled into bed. I am sure she's utterly exhausted." Anne yawned. She didn't know what exhausted meant, but she sure was hardly able to hold her head up, she was so tired.

John had come in toting pieces of the bed frame up the stairs, his tool belt slung about his waist. From upstairs, they could hear hammering and the bumping sound of wood being shifted and placed. Henry's eyes grew wide, and he began spooning soup into his mouth even faster.

"Now, now, Henry," Mary said, "Slow down just a bit. Can't have you choking on your food here at the table." Henry slowed down for just a moment, and then spooned fast again. He just had to get up those stairs and see how Uncle John was putting the bed together. Mary understood his eagerness and caught his eye. Connecting with him eye to eye, she raised an eyebrow and pointedly glanced at his spoon. Henry understood and slowed down once more.

"Sorry, Aunt Mary," he mumbled sheepishly and worked hard to use all his manners eating the rest of his food.

In no time at all, everything was settled upstairs.

Anne was washed and scrubbed and dressed in clean bedclothes. Henry, also, had been scrubbed within an inch of his life. His young face glowed, shiny and clean. He was now helping Uncle John place the blackout boards in all the windows while Jane and Anne were upstairs with Mary. Mary was tucking Anne into her new bed.

"Here at Orchard Glen Farm, we like to pray before bed and sometimes sing a bit of a hymn," Mary was explaining to the small girl, with Jane nodding alongside her. Mary sat down in the rocking chair that was now placed against the wall between the two beds in the room. Anne was tucked under Mary's handmade quilt. Jane sat at Mary's feet; she wasn't quite ready to go to bed. She would go down with Aunt Mary to the living room after Anne was all tucked in. Aunt Mary began to sing. It was a hymn Jane was just beginning to come to know; Anne didn't know it at all. Although prayers and hymns were a natural way of life for John and Mary, war or no war, that wasn't the case for many. Yet, during these uncertain days, many in England were turning to faith for comfort, guidance. Mary knew that any truth she could impress upon these young hearts would stay with them through all the days of their lives, a pillar of strength laid down in a foundation of truth. She took a deep breath and began to sing:

How sweet the Name of Jesus sounds
In a believer's ear!
It soothes his sorrows, heals his wounds,
And drives away his fear.
It makes the wounded spirit whole,
And calms the troubled breast;
'Tis manna to the hungry soul,
And to the weary, rest.
Dear Name, the Rock on which I build,
My Shield and Hiding Place,
My never failing treasury, filled
With boundless stores of grace!

Aunt Mary's gentle voice filled the room, and Jane closed her eyes, resting her head against the bed frame. Jesus could drive away her fear. She pondered the words carefully. She thought about the anxiety she hadn't been able to share with Aunt Mary earlier in the day; suddenly, her belly clenched tight. Somehow, the Lord could calm a troubled heart. He would make it clear to her; she knew He would.

Jane opened her eyes as Aunt Mary finished the prayer. Little Anne was already asleep. Soothed by the song and the lulling words of the prayer, she was completely out. Mary stood up and smoothed the hair off Anne's forehead. "Precious mite," she whispered, and she and Jane quietly left the room and gently closed the door.

5

Peace Which Passeth All Understanding

August 20, 1940

Jane woke up one morning just a week later. She blinked as the sunlight washed across her face. Sitting up, she looked across the room to Anne's bed. There she was, curled up into a little ball, with one hand tucked under her cheek. Jane smiled. Little by little, Anne was getting used to Orchard Glen Farm. Yesterday, she had even laughed out loud when Henry had to chase a chicken all over the farmyard. Suddenly, Jane paused and frowned. Anne had told her that her Dad left when she was a baby, and from what she mentioned, it didn't seem like her Mum was around that much. Anne and Aunt Mary had worked to send the letter off to home, but Anne hadn't said much other than that she didn't know when her Mum might ever come to visit. She had a pinched look about her face when she said it, and Jane's heart hurt.

Jane swung her legs over the side of the bed. It was time to get up. Today they were all heading out to the field to help Uncle John bring in the "second early" potato crop. She stretched and smiled. Uncle John planned to try out the new tractor he brought back from town.

As Jane's feet gently hit the floor, Anne woke up. She crinkled her eyebrows and looked a bit confused. She sometimes still woke up not remembering where she was. Jane saw her and cheerfully but quietly said, "Good morning, Anne! It's potato harvest day."

"Good morning," Anne answered sleepily and sat up, too.

"Let's hurry and get down to breakfast." The girls dressed quickly and headed down to the kitchen. They met Henry on the stairs. He was bouncing with boyish enthusiasm. A tractor sure was exciting!

"Hi, Henry!" Jane called, and they all bounded down together.

Mary smiled at the children as they entered the kitchen. "Good morning, my lovelies! Come help set the table. We've got eggs and bread and jam this morning." She poured frothy milk into three cups, one for each child. At the counter, she was packing bread with savory cottage cheese into packages for a quick lunch out in the field. "Uncle John's already taken the tractor out to the field; he took our hoes, too. We'll just gather up our buckets and be off."

In no time, they were all trudging out across the field in the warm, bright August sunlight. They found Uncle John already on the tractor, turning up the potatoes row by row. Quickly, they all went to work, bending down and plucking upturned potatoes, placing them in the buckets. It was dirty work, and soon all hands were brown and caked.

Uncle John stopped the tractor for a moment and called to Henry, "Would you like to ride up with me, Henry?"

"Yes, I sure would," Henry answered, but Jane gave him a nudge with her elbow. He looked at her and "Hey!" slipped out of his mouth until he saw that Jane was gesturing furiously at Anne, a couple rows over next to Aunt Mary. Anne clearly longed for a ride on the big tractor; she was watching Uncle John with those big, blue eyes. Henry swallowed hard. He knew what he needed to do. "Uncle John, how 'bout you take Anne first? She looks like she'd really like a ride."

Anne looked over in total surprise.

Uncle John's smile looked like it would split the sky. "Why, Henry, that's a fine idea! How 'bout it,

Anne?" he called over to the small girl.

"Oh, yes! Yes, please!" Anne squeaked out and hurried over the uneven ground to the tractor. Aunt Mary raised her up, and Uncle John swung her up right next to him. Anne couldn't stop smiling, and she grabbed onto Uncle John's arm for safety as the tractor roared and snorted forward. She snuggled in close. Anne looked so small next to Uncle John on that big tractor.

Aunt Mary stepped back, away from the machine, with her hand shielding the sun from her eyes and her heart full. She turned toward Henry, who had pressed his lips into a thin line and had his face to the dirt, pulling potatoes. "Why, Henry, that was a lovely thing to do."

"'Twas Jane's idea," he muttered in a low voice.

"That doesn't matter," Aunt Mary said gently. "You're the one who chose to act. My, how strong you are growing inside to make such a good choice for someone else."

Henry looked up at Aunt Mary and thought a

bit. "I guess it's hard to be strong inside, but it sure feels good to do what's right," he said after a moment. Jane smiled.

That evening they all gathered in the living room. The blackout panels were all in place, and candles glimmered cheerily, casting golden shadows. Aunt Mary had her head bent next to Anne's as she showed her how to form a knit stitch with the knitting needles. Jane was tucked up in the corner of a chair while Henry worked on a small carving project. Out here in the country, the children could almost forget about the threat of bombs and war. Uncle John turned the wireless on, and a speech from the Prime Minister came out over the speaker. It was August 20, 1940, and the warfare was increasing. Jane started listening carefully; Prime Minister Churchill was speaking about the airmen. Terrified, Jane realized he was telling about the grave danger the British fighter pilots faced every day, and how much was owed to their skill and bravery; he was actually saying

Peace Which Passeth All Understanding

that the victory of the whole war might be owed to the pilots. Suddenly, Jane choked. She knew Father was up there in the skies. Why, he might be up there right at this very minute, heading into dangerous German territory, using all his skill to avoid death and destruction. She couldn't stand the thought. She felt like she couldn't breathe. She jumped up. Grabbing the candleholder nearest her, she hurried from the room and up the stairs to the bedroom. The candle shadows made everything look long and skinny, and she set the holder down on the little table. Face down, she pressed her body into her bed and tried to breathe.

She felt the bed give a little, and Aunt Mary's comforting presence pressed close.

"Jane, dear," Aunt Mary said as she smoothed the hair behind Jane's ear, "I know you've been suffering for a while." Jane stiffened deeper into the covers. She felt so anxious and tight inside, she couldn't even cry. She could hardly breathe. Aunt Mary was patting her back, and then she started to hum a hymn under her breath. Jane began to feel just a bit better. She rolled onto her side.

"Aunt Mary, I don't feel well," she said in a small voice.

Aunt Mary rubbed her back a bit more. "Jane, dear, our Heavenly Father can help. His grace is available to you, and you can access it through the Holy Scriptures and prayer."

"I don't know how. I get so tight inside, I can't think straight. I can't eat. I sometimes feel like I can't breathe." She barely squeezed out the words.

"Jane, our merciful Lord knows you fully; He knows everything about you inside and out, and nothing is a surprise to Him. He can help you with your thoughts. Did you know that He promises peace beyond understanding? When the troubles start to multiply in your heart and mind, take them to the Lord. You can write them out to Him or pray out loud to Him. You can do this again and again, as many times in a day or an hour as needed. And then, the next thing is just to do the task at hand.

The very motion of doing the next thing can help dislodge the body and mind from the squeeze of anxiety."

Jane was listening carefully; the very sound of Mary's gentle voice was soothing the storm inside her. She looked up at Aunt Mary with huge, wet, gray eyes. Mary smiled down at her.

"What's my next thing to do now, Aunt Mary?" Jane asked quietly. She was going to take one step to help calm this inner storm down.

"I think it's to get to bed. We'll get Anne and Henry up here and have some songs. Why don't you wash up and do what's needed for bedtime? It's certainly been a long and busy day. I'll be back in a minute."

That night Jane lay looking up at the now very familiar ceiling of her room at Orchard Glen Farm. Anne's gentle breathing thrummed in the air. Jane was thinking hard. There was still so much to learn about the Lord and His great love. She never really knew that He cared to help her with her own thoughts and terrified inward struggles. Finally, she had let Aunt Mary know about her burden. She gave a deep sigh and buried deeper into the pillow. She really wasn't alone. The lines from Mary's hymn filled her mind:

> *How sweet the Name of Jesus sounds*
> *In a believer's ear!*
> *It soothes his sorrows, heals his wounds,*
> *And drives away his fear.*

6

Letters from London

Autumn 1940

The children sat around the kitchen table eating apples. Mary had several letters in her hand. She handed the first one to Jane. Henry leaned in.

"Will you read it out to us, Aunt Mary?" Jane asked after she had taken a moment to treasure Mummy's neat, black scrawl flowing over the pages.

"Of course, Jane," Aunt Mary said, and she sat down next to the children with the letter in hand.

Hello to everyone at Orchard Glen Farm!

    I write to you from the bustle of London. It's amazing to see the courage of the people. We are all working together to endure for Britain's sake.

    Mary has written to me of how you have expanded the farm, are reusing and recycling everything possible, and are finding creative ways to manage shortages. Jane, you would be so delighted to see the victory garden I have planted in the little plot nearby. Gardens have sprung up everywhere here in London. Even the king has had war gardens planted at Buckingham Palace and Windsor Castle. Have you seen the posters in your village? "Dig for Victory" is the motto, and everyone is pitching in. We are all determined to endure for Britain's sake.

    I cannot write without letting you know how things really are here in London. I don't want you to hear about the London bombings on the wireless and worry for me. It's quite usual now for air raid sirens to be on at all times, day or night.

Last night, I woke to the sound of the air raid siren coming to me from out of the darkness. Don't fear; I am not alone. Our neighbors the Hentleys have joined arms with me. We managed to get into the Anderson shelter together, and we made a plan to spend nights in the Underground for a while to come. The Underground is the safest place to be right now at night. The Germans have begun what are being called Lightning Raids, or the Blitz. You might have heard about it on the wireless. They are no longer bombing as much during the daytime.

    Mrs. Hentley has been working with me in the Women's Volunteer Service (WVS). We've been able to provide a lot of comfort to many people: food, clothes, shelter, and more. Should anything happen to our home, I intend to come to Orchard Glen Farm, as I know Uncle John and Aunt Mary have warmly invited me so often. I will put forth my efforts for the home front from the farm, if that may be the case.

    I had a letter from Father just a day or so ago. He is facing more intense action these days. The whole face of our combat is directed to the Royal Air Force. Jane and Henry, think of your Dad and be proud! He bravely serves Britain.

    My, this letter has gotten long. I am safe, dear ones, and serving Britain! Much work to be done everywhere. I will see you soon.

Love,

Helen (Mummy)

Jane looked at the window. Streaks of white clouds feathered through the blue sky. Everything lush and green. Last night she slept peacefully in her bed at Orchard Glen Farm. Where was Mummy? Sheltered down in the Underground? And Dad? She shuddered. Her heart was torn in two: how she loved Orchard Glen Farm but how she missed Mummy and Dad. Henry squeezed her hand. Jane knew he understood just how she was feeling. Gently, he leaned into her just a bit.

Anne had a letter, too. It was from her mum. She was leaving London and going abroad to Canada; she didn't know when she would be back.

Dear Anne,

I hope you are keeping your chin up and doing your part. I am leaving London to go abroad, away from this terrible war. I will travel on September 20th. I will already be gone by the time you receive this letter. Do your best for Mr. and Mrs. Stuart. Don't cause trouble. I will write and let you know an address when I have one.

Love,

Mum

Mary found Anne crying into her pillow later that evening. She was stifling her sobs in the feather-stuffed pillow.

"Anne, dear," she murmured and pulled the small girl onto her lap. "I'm so glad you're here with us. You'll always have a home at Orchard Glen Farm. We'll do all we can to keep you safe with us."

"Really?" Anne raised a tear-stained face in the darkness. "My mum, she never seems to care that much. I don't know when I'll see her again."

Mary didn't say anything for a bit. Her heart ached hard for the small, suffering girl. "I want to tell you a bit more about our Lord, Anne. Did you know that He promises to never leave you or forsake you? Psalm 27:10 teaches that even if our father or mother forsakes us, He will take us up. Uncle John and I want to live out that love so you can know it in your head, but feel it in your life, too."

Anne listened. "Can you sing me the hymn again, Aunt Mary? The one about Jesus driving away the fear?"

"Of course, dear." Mary began to sing the hymn that she had been singing every night since Anne arrived, and the verses filled the room with comfort and truth. Anne leaned against her shoulder.

How sweet the Name of Jesus sounds
In a believer's ear!
It soothes his sorrows, heals his wounds,
And drives away his fear.
It makes the wounded spirit whole,
And calms the troubled breast;
'Tis manna to the hungry soul,
And to the weary, rest.
Dear Name, the Rock on which I build,
My Shield and Hiding Place,
My never failing treasury, filled
With boundless stores of grace!

Anne sighed in relief, her breathing coming more easily and her tormented face easing into greater peace.

"Do you think you can come back down now, dear? Uncle John's got a crackling fire going in the grate, and we can work on your knitting project a bit more before bed."

"I think so, Aunt Mary," Anne answered and brushed herself off.

"I'll just be down in a minute," Aunt Mary offered as Anne left the room.

Truth was, Mary wasn't feeling too well. She broke out in a small sweat while singing. With great, tender patience, she managed to finish speaking to Anne and then slipped away to splash cold water on her face. My, she didn't feel well. She hadn't been feeling well for days. Perhaps she could slip away to town to see Mr. Goldwell, the doctor. She didn't want John or the children to worry. She had an errand to run anyway; she could just combine both. She'd see about it in a day or so.

7

Aunt Mary Goes to Town

John and Mary were together in the kitchen at the end of the day several days later. The children were all tucked in, and they had come to close out the day. Mary leaned weakly against the wall. John came over with a frown between his eyes.

"Let's 'ave a cup of tea, shall we? You look all tuckered out." He lit the gas stove for the ready kettle and held out the chair for Mary. She sank into it gratefully, looking pale around the edges.

"Truth is, John, I haven't been feeling well at all lately. It seems to be getting worse. I thought I could just press through. I'd like to take Chester and Ginger into town tomorrow. I wanted to see about the Women's Institute. Joining the WI would be such a wonderful way to serve the village; there is always so much to do. I felt so inspired by Helen's mention of the WVS she is supporting in London. We can do our part, here, too. And I'll just step in to see Mr. Goldwell. I don't want to worry the children. I didn't want to worry you, but I know you need to know." A tear slipped out of her eye. She felt so weary to the bone.

John sat down next to her and pulled her into his arm against his shoulder. She pressed her head into the crook of his arm; his shoulder always seemed made just for her.

"I'll help get the children off to school in the morning and work near the house tomorrow so you can get off first thing."

The children had just started back to school

now that the harvest was in. Even little Anne was experiencing her first days in the schoolhouse, and she was so excited to learn to read. Inadvertently, both John and Mary smiled, thinking of the children neat and washed, carrying their lunch pails and traipsing off together.

"Thank you, John," Mary said, and then she sighed. John grasped her hand in a gentle squeeze. His work-rough hand closed around her hand, and another tear trickled out of her eye.

The whistle on the tea kettle started singing merrily. John grinned and turned to retrieve the steaming kettle. He poured gentle, herbal mint tea dried from their own garden for the both of them. Mary sipped hers slowly, leaning again against John. She felt the comfort of his strength and the tenderness of his love. Resting in the crook of his arm, she felt relieved and free because she shared her trouble. The morning would come soon enough, and then it would be time to face the day.

Finishing up their tea, they headed up to bed.

Kneeling together, once more, John prayed for Mary specifically. Together, they prayed carefully for Helen and William, for Anne's mother, for all of England, Prime Minister Churchill, and the war effort. They prayed for evil to be stopped and for right to prevail. They prayed for protection from the Blitz, from any bombs dropping, for all of England.

The next morning dawned bright with sunshine and birdsong. John was in the kitchen at first light, helping get breakfast sorted. He had Ginger and Chester ready and waiting for Mary to step into the cart. At first, Jane didn't notice anything unusual as she came down to the kitchen. Then, she saw Mary all dressed in going-to-town clothes. Suddenly, she wondered why Uncle John was in the kitchen and not out at the barn. She knew Henry was already out with the chickens, tending them with Anne alongside helping.

"Good morning, Uncle John, Aunt Mary? Is something happening today?" she asked with wide eyes as she encountered them both in the kitchen.

"Aye," Uncle John answered, "Aunt Mary's off to town to see about the Women's Institute and get some things checked out. Could be that you'll be able to work with her to help the village. I've heard they're canning vegetables and making jam for the war effort like you wouldn't believe." He chuckled, and Jane was successfully diverted from any concern. Lately, Aunt Mary had been teaching her to can, and she had experienced some interesting trials. She hadn't always had such great success. Her eyes widened. She thought of a recent incident when she hadn't sealed the jar correctly before it was placed into the water bath. She had enough to concentrate on learning to cook!

"I'd like to help out with the WI," Jane said with a gulp.

Aunt Mary was placing the lunches into the tins for everyone. She looked over and caught Jane's eye with a smile. "That'd be grand," she said heartily. Jane couldn't help herself; she started to giggle. Mary laughed out loud, and John chuckled his familiar low rumble.

"That's how we learn, that's for sure. Sometimes, by our mistakes," John said sagely. Jane nodded with just a bit of a flush in her creamy cheeks.

Henry and Anne came in with a basket full of eggs and set them over at the wash station. Henry managed to keep clean, and his blond hair was slicked down except for one wayward strand. Anne carefully washed her hands, her blue eyes glimmering from the fresh air and sunshine and vigor of the early morning.

"Come, let's eat," Uncle John called. "Aunt Mary's going to head out now. I'll see you off to school. I'll just step out to help her get settled into the carriage. Get washed up if you haven't already." He smiled at Anne. "I'll be back right quick." John followed Mary out the door to where the cart and driver were waiting. He gave her a hand and helped her up. She settled into the cart. She was slight and her blond hair shone in the sun. Her blue eyes were tinged with a bit of gray. The fatigue she tried so hard to hide peeked out in the shadows around her eyes.

"Thank you, John," she said quietly.

He looked up at her tenderly, noting how pale she looked and wondering how he could have missed it for so long. "Safe travels. I'm prayin' for you, and I know all will be well."

Mary smiled at him, giving him one last look. With a jostle, she was off down the road and away into town.

John turned back into the house. A bit of a storm cloud rested on his brow. Concern for Mary flooded his mind, and he frowned, thinking hard. He turned resolutely toward the house. Despite his concern for Mary, he couldn't help the grin that broke out across his face. It sure was great fun helping these children off to school. How dapper they were, all shined up and ready for the day. Time to see that they got enough eggs and toast and jam and tea. Days could be long for the young sprites. He didn't usually get to see them set off all together for the schoolhouse. It was a bright spot amidst his concern for Mary.

Aunt Mary Goes to Town

{ 177 }

8

The Women's Institute

Mary traveled on to meet up with Susan Holmes, the woman in charge of the WI. She would see about joining and then stop by Mr. Goldwell's. Mary knew there was a knitting meeting being held at Susan's home. After the driver pulled Chester and Ginger to a stop outside the cottage, Mary climbed down and tethered them. Susan's front door was open, and Mary peered around the doorframe and rapped cheerily.

"Hullo, Susan? It's Mary from Orchard Glen Farm." Through the doorway, Mary could see a group of women gathered together, bent over needles and yarn. Susan Holmes came to the doorway, a delighted smile lighting her face.

"Why, hullo, Mary! How can I help?" she asked.

"I've come to see about joining the WI. I was hoping I could be a part, and perhaps our Jane and Anne—they're the evacuees from London we're housing at the farm—could help, too. We'd like to do our bit."

"Why, that's wonderful," Susan beamed. "Our next meeting is just around the corner. We'll be working together with the WVS to prepare and distribute pies all through the countryside to the farmers and Women's Land Army. How does that sound to you?"

Mary smiled. "I'd love to be a part. Thank you."

Susan turned and went swiftly inside. She returned with a flyer that she handed to Mary. "We'll be meeting at the Village Hall at 10 a.m. on

Saturday, October 26th."

"How's it all going for you today?" Mary inquired warmly.

"Oh, fine, it is," Susan replied. "We're doing our part to 'Make Do and Mend,'" she added with a smile. "All sorts of projects going on." She beckoned over her shoulder. Mary could see some smiles and nods. She smiled back and gave a little wave. Susan continued with satisfaction: "Sweaters, socks, hats, scarves, blankets. Anything for a bit of comfort."

"We've been working on knitting at the farm," Mary offered. "We can contribute, too. I'll bring a few items to the next meeting."

"That'd be grand!" Susan said enthusiastically.

"Well, I'll let you get back to it," Mary said. "I'm off to another errand."

With another cheerful wave and words of good wishes, Mary nodded and smiled and made her way back to the cart. Off to Mr. Goldwell's. She couldn't help it—her belly clenched with nerves. She turned her mind to the Lord and tried to recall a verse or hymn. Quietly, she recited Psalm 121:7 out loud: *The Lord shall preserve thee from all evil: he shall preserve thy soul.* Taking a deep breath, she cast her mind on the Lord and asked Him to help her rest in Him.

9

Be Anxious for Nothing

Jane was outside in Aunt Mary's rose garden, tending the plants carefully. She was bundled up in a wool coat and tights. Around her neck, the tails of a red knitted scarf lifted gently in the brisk November wind. With a smile that tugged at the corners of her mouth, Jane rubbed a bit of the wool between her fingers. The scarf was a gift made just for her from Anne. Anne had worked so hard on the scarf, tearing out row after row until she learned how to knit without dropping a stitch. The brilliant red gift was hard-earned, and Jane felt proud to wear it. The color flamed against the dark wool like the flicker of a robin's belly in flight across the moody November sky.

With a keen eye, Jane was removing dead petals and pinching off any leaves that looked unhealthy. Aunt Mary had talked about moving some bushes to different locations. Jane stood studying the layout carefully. She stopped for a minute, deep in thought. Aunt Mary was inside, resting just as she had been every afternoon since she came home from her trip to town weeks ago. Jane could

still hardly believe the news. She grinned. Such a delightful surprise coming to the farm! Aunt Mary was going to have a baby in the spring. The tumult that erupted at the farm when Aunt Mary arrived home, pale and a bit wobbly, was beyond anything Jane had ever experienced in a family. Such joy! Uncle John stood speechless. Then, he had to sit down in a chair. Aunt Mary couldn't wait to share the shocking information Mr. Goldwell had given her, and she just blurted everything out all at once. Henry had stood next to Uncle John's chair and put a manly young hand on his shoulder as if to give him strength to carry on. Jane and Anne had squealed with joy. Somehow, the children all knew how much a baby meant to Aunt Mary and Uncle John. Maybe it was the love that enfolded them all day in and day out; maybe it was the tender care they experienced in every interaction. They just knew that this baby was a mighty answer to prayer and completely unexpected. A wartime baby. A gift in the trial. Even so, Aunt Mary really wasn't feeling well, and everyone was pitching in to try to give her more rest.

"Jane!" Henry was coming from the house. "We've had a letter from Mother. Come on in so we can read it." Reaching her side, a little breathless, Henry looked up at Jane's face. He seemed to get taller by the day.

"All right," she replied. She had just finished with the roses. Together they walked from the rose garden down the path to the kitchen door. The gray stone on the path crunched under their sturdy shoes. Jane tried to take deep, calming breaths. The anxious swirling in her belly was trying to overtake her. Inside her mind, she tried to recite Philippians 4:6–7: *Be careful for nothing; but in every thing by prayer and supplication with thanksgiving let your requests be made known unto God. And the peace of God, which passeth all understanding, shall keep your hearts and minds through Christ Jesus.*

"I'm glad we've had a letter, Henry. I love to hear from Mummy," Jane bravely spoke out the words in the cold November air. Henry squeezed her hand. He understood.

Together, Jane and Henry walked through to the living room. Mary and John were there with Anne seated nearby.

"We've had a letter, Jane," Mary said happily. Letters were a big occurrence. Receiving one could be happy or terrifying during these difficult days. Mary tried to always hope for the best to keep a spirit of doom from frightening the children. Each one had to learn how to step through each day, one at a time. Never knowing what a day may hold never seemed more real than during wartime.

Uncle John held the letter out and began to read it:

"Dear John, Mary, Jane, Henry, and sweet Anne,"

(Mother always remembered Anne, Jane thought. She's so thoughtful. She looked over at Anne, who straightened when she realized the letter was for her, too. Jane felt proud and glad to have Mummy as her own. Jane wriggled. Mummy didn't know about the baby yet. Oh! She couldn't wait for her to find out.)

Uncle John was reading the letter, and Jane was about to miss it. She focused her attention.

I hope all is well at Orchard Glen Farm. I have some terrible news that I hoped I would never have to share. Several nights ago, on one of the fiercest nights of the Blitz, our London home was bombed and completely destroyed. As you know, the Germans have moved to almost completely bombing the cities at nighttime, and I have taken to sheltering in the Underground with the Hentleys.

I am relieved to say that I am completely safe and no harm was done to me, but I am ready to come to Orchard Glen Farm for the duration. I have done all the good here in London I can do for now. I have sent a letter off to Father already, children. So he is aware, and he knows that the farm is where he should come if he should ever get leave or when this horrible war finally ends. I will be there in just days. The WVS has provided me some necessary items—food and other essentials—and I will salvage everything I can from the rubble. I'm looking desperately forward to seeing you all and deeply saddened over the loss of our home. Pray for Father; pray for me. I'll be there soon.

Yours,
Helen (Mummy)

Everyone sat still and silent for a moment. Jane realized her cheeks were wet. How glad she was that Mummy was safe—but their home? Smashed to bits forever. Henry smooshed close to her, and in that moment, all the tallness she felt outside in the rose garden disappeared; he felt small, huddled next to her. She linked her arm in his.

Uncle John cleared his throat. "Jane, Henry," he began, "you've known all along we've wanted to welcome your entire family to Orchard Glen Farm. I am deeply sorry that you've lost your London home, but I know I speak for Mary, too . . ." and he looked at Mary next to him. She smiled up into his eyes. ". . . when I say that we are blessed to have a place your mum can come to, and we hope she and you will find comfort here during this time with us."

"Try not to be scared," Mary began. "Remember, Mummy is safe and on her way. Father is safe, too, as far as we know."

"I know, Aunt Mary," Jane said in a very small voice. Henry squeezed her arm. Anne hopped up and came over to Jane. She put her arm around the back of her neck.

"It's okay, Jane," Anne whispered. Jane smiled at Anne through bright eyes. She wanted to be the comfort to Anne through these difficult days, yet here was Anne, comforting her. With a flash, she realized how blessed she was.

"Let's get on with getting ready for teatime," Uncle John said. "A bit of nourishment will do us all good." Mary smiled and stood up slowly. Moving too quickly made her dizzy. John grabbed her by the hand. Henry bounded forward, and evening chores began.

That night, Mary and John were tucked together in the corner of the couch. Mary was resting against his shoulder. The room was shrouded in the heavy darkness that only came from blackout. Several fat candles flickered, casting warm shadows.

"I'm glad Helen is on her way. Having her here removes the daily concern that she might be caught in an explosion or injured in an air raid," Mary murmured the words quietly. The children were tucked in upstairs, but she didn't want her words to carry and cause worry.

"Aye," John agreed. With his arm around Mary, he felt he was holding his greatest earthly treasure, and he still couldn't quite believe they were going to have a child of their own. The days were unusual in so many ways—a miracle war baby on the way, more guests to welcome at the farm, more farm production than he ever imagined possible—his mind could barely take it in! Through it all—the hard and the good—he felt joy in his soul that witnessed the hand of the Lord in their midst.

After a pause, Mary offered in a thin voice: "I haven't been feeling well at all, John. I can't seem to keep up with the work needed on the farm."

"No need to worry now, Mary. No one feels you're not doing enough at all. Jane and Henry and Anne and I, well, we're all glad to do our part and more. You're doing a mighty big job in itself, with growing a baby."

"I never knew I'd feel so exhausted. Sometimes I wonder if something isn't quite right. I've got the antenatal clinics every month. So far, all checks out. Eventually, the midwife will be coming out."

John listened carefully. He understood her concern. They had longed for a baby for so long that it didn't seem real or right sometimes that they were really going to have their own. The pregnancy itself was a journey of its own: an incredible blessing, yet requiring much. "It's hard not to worry and borrow trouble," he said, "especially during these days when the news reports and wireless bring new sanctions and troubles and needs. Remember the Scriptures we encourage the children with to set their minds on things above. We have the promise of Christ's peace. It's hard sometimes to keep the mind on what is good and true and beautiful, but doing so really is an act of trust: trusting yourself into the Lord's good hands. No safer place you can be, Mary." He leaned in and kissed the top of her golden head. Mary sighed softly. She knew John was right.

10

Christmas Surprise

December 1940

Mummy arrived on the farm just in time. With luggage in hand and a jaunty hat askew on the side of her head, her stalwart attitude blew through Orchard Glen Farm like a wind whisking dust and cobwebs away. Taking one look at Mary, she immediately discerned what was needed. Mary needed a lot of help, and Helen was delighted to pitch in and serve at Orchard Glen Farm. In no time, Mary was more comfortable, Orchard Glen

Farm was under serene order again, and Jane, Henry, and Anne were pitching in and learning lots of new tasks. Jane was thrilled. Having Mummy at Orchard Glen Farm for good was one of her most dearly held hopes come true. The only thing better would be having Daddy here, too. Henry seemed to bounce with even more energy, his hair and eyes electric with liveliness. Even though neither child could really admit it out loud, a huge burden was lifted by having Mummy safe with them in the countryside.

Anne, too, basked in the kindness of the grown women around her. Both Mary and Helen seemed to know just when the little girl needed to be challenged and when she needed to be nurtured.

Every day, Anne was learning more about God's great love. She watched how tenderly Uncle John cared for Aunt Mary, and she was privy to some conversations about faith and trust between Aunt Mary and Mrs. Townsend. God's great world was opening up to her like the domed sky that curved over Orchard Glen Farm, immense in scope, awe, and beauty. She had learned to read a bit by now, and Aunt Mary read Scriptures to her. Anne helped her read some of the small words, so really they were reading together. Aunt Mary was especially working with her on Psalm 121. Jane and Henry were learning the verses by heart, too.

Everyone at Orchard Glen Farm was getting ready for their second wartime Christmas. The restrictions were felt even more this year, and everything possible would be made by hand. All over the country, people were determined to celebrate the season. Christmas was one holiday still celebrated, despite so much being shut down or restricted because of the war effort.

Helen was helping Mary decorate just the way she liked it. Helen knew the comfort it brought to have traditions and household duties completed just the way they ought to be. Mary would tell, and Helen would do. Little bits of tin foil were twisted to make sparkling decorations, and wartime recipes were collected to create different but festive foods for the meal. As secretly as they could, Mary and Helen were making soap as a surprise gift for everyone. Soap was hard to come by these days, and everyone, even Henry, would be delighted with a bar for Christmas.

Uncle John and Henry had been working out a surprise, too, for months now. For ever so long, they had been holed up in the barn whenever they could, working on a special secret. Henry could hardly keep the plan to himself, but somehow he managed.

* * *

Jane woke up on Christmas Eve morning, tingling with excitement. She couldn't help herself, and she leaned over the side of her bed, whispering, "Anne! Anne! Are you up?"

Anne opened her eyes and grinned at Jane.

"It's Christmas Eve! We'll have the candlelight service at church this evening and a special meal for tea. I think Uncle John and Henry are presenting their surprise, too." Jane was up and dressing quickly as she chattered. The air was cold and frosty, and Jane was bundling up.

Anne was up, too. Wide-eyed, she was thinking through all the excitement. She had never really celebrated Christmas before. Everything was new for her at Orchard Glen Farm.

Hurrying into the kitchen, they found steaming cups of raspberry tea and toast waiting for them. Mummy was slicing bread. They had an extra bit of ham this morning to celebrate the special day. Aunt Mary was putting ingredients into a soup pot. Tonight, they would enjoy a meal of savory soup and bread by candlelight before the service.

"Oh, I can hardly wait for tonight!" Jane was up on her tiptoes in excitement, with little Anne following suit.

"Uncle John and Henry have a surprise ready for us after all the chores are done, so hopefully that will make the time go a bit faster." As she said this, Mary looked at Helen with a knowing glance. Days drag long for expectant children sometimes.

Jane and Henry: A World War II Adventure: A Sequel

Christmas Surprise

After breakfast, the children helped wash up and then joined in the work to put the house to rights, tend the animals, and prepare for the evening meal. As soon as everything was satisfactorily tucked away, Uncle John and Henry mysteriously disappeared. They returned carrying a box stuffed with straw.

"Merry Christmas!" Henry cried, and he placed the box on the kitchen table. "There is something inside for everyone to open. Anne gets to go first." He smiled at her.

Anne reached into the box and pulled out a small brown bundle, tightly wrapped. She pulled apart the wrapping and discovered a carved wooden donkey.

"Oh!" she breathed and held the wooden creation carefully in her small hand; it fit perfectly. Next it was Jane's turn. She reached into the box. Unwrapping her bundle, she revealed a small manger. She held it up for everyone to see. Carefully, she placed it on the table.

"It's your turn, Helen," John said with a lilt of joy.

Helen reached into the box and unearthed a bundle that turned out to be a shepherd. "This is wonderful work," she said, examining the figure carefully. The collection of figures was growing on the kitchen table.

"Aunt Mary, you're next!" Henry was up on his tippy toes with excitement. Boy, this was fun! Everyone was so pleased.

Mary reached in and withdrew a small, carefully wrapped package. She pulled the paper apart and found a small model of the baby Jesus. She held the baby carefully in her palm, her eyes filling with tears. "Baby Jesus," she whispered—a miracle baby in her hand. She felt the baby tucked safe in her womb give a couple of quick flutters. The Christmas story, and especially Mary the mother of Jesus' story, was deeply close and precious to her heart right now. She placed the baby carefully into the manger Jane had unwrapped.

Uncle John looked at Henry. "Go on, young man. You can have a turn, too."

"Oh, thank you, Uncle John!" Henry exclaimed. He reached in and pulled out one of the bigger parcels. Unwrapping it, he revealed a carefully carved angel.

One by one, the entire contents of the box were unwrapped and a hand-carved nativity stood displayed on the kitchen table.

"It's wonderful!" Helen exclaimed.

"Now," said John, "Henry and I have prepared something extra special to go 'long with this nativity set." He pulled out a piece of paper. "I've gathered the verses in order that tell the Christmas story. I wondered if you'd all like to go around one by one and tell the story through these verses and put the nativity in order as we go. We'll need to share Bibles. I thought we could begin now, perhaps read some more after teatime, and then finish the Scriptures tomorrow. I do think it's a bit long to try to do it all in one go." John frowned a little. He didn't want the children to have trouble paying attention. "I thought we could display the figures on the fireplace mantel in the living room. I worked out the best order in the readings for placement. We can place them up in order as we go through the verses."

"Oh, John," Mary breathed. "What a wonderful idea!"

Carefully, Henry placed all the figures back into the box and carried it into the living room.

Anne was so excited. The Christmas story! She loved the mystery, the joy, and the love all mixed together. At school, they had been practicing a pageant, and she had gotten to be a small angel. Anne had learned to say: "Fear not, for behold, I bring you tidings of great joy to all people!" as loud as she could with her arms spread wide like wings.

As Uncle John gathered everyone and began to read from Matthew 1:18, Anne was waiting and ready, sitting on the edge of her chair. She would get to be the first person to place a figure up on the mantel. She was holding the stable in her hand. Henry would go next, and he had the manger in his.

Together, they worked through the verses one by one. For Anne and Henry, Uncle John would read a section of their verse out loud and they would repeat after him, since the verses were too difficult for them to read easily. They made it through Luke 2 verse 7, and everyone had a chance to place a figure up on the mantel.

Uncle John closed his Bible. "We'll do more tonight or finish the story altogether tomorrow. It's time to have a quick bite to eat, tend to the animals again, and get ready for church this evening. We'll sit down in our church clothes for our Christmas Eve tea." Mary looked at John with a light in her eyes and a smile curving across her face. Dressing up for this meal made it feel all the more special. It was Anne's first Christmas at Orchard Glen Farm, and Mary knew he wanted her to know what to expect. He would lead a Christmas carol at the start, too, Mary knew. Oh, how she loved everything about it! Lines from the familiar, rousing Sussex Christmas Carol filled her mind:

Then why should men on earth be so sad,
Since our Redeemer made us glad,
When from our sin He set us free,
All for to gain our liberty?
When sin departs before His grace,
Then life and health come in its place.
Angels and men with joy may sing
All for to see the new-born King.
All out of darkness we have light,
Which made the angels sing this night:
"Glory to God and peace to men,
Now and for evermore, Amen!"

Mary thought for a moment. How the Lord brought comfort and peace, even in difficult times. He Himself, all joy and light.

As Jane got up to go on to her chores, she sighed in deep delight. The Scriptures sank down in her heart; how nice it was to hear everyone's voices reading out the verses one by one. The familiar tones from each person, so dear to her, in the room brought comfort and peace to her heart. She looked around the living room. Aunt Mary and Mummy had done so much to make it festive; she and Anne had helped, too. Greenery was hung cheerily about the windows and the mantel. Fat red candles were tucked here and there. Silvery foil decorations, twirled by Mummy, hung from the room corners. How she loved Christmas! There was nothing, just nothing, like taking the time to realize that Jesus actually came to earth to be the Savior of the world![1]

---

1   See Appendix for Uncle John's full Christmas Nativity Program.

11

The Lord Is My Light and My Salvation, Whom Shall I Fear?

One afternoon, Mummy was sitting at the kitchen table with a letter from Father in hand. Jane found her there as she came in from school. Mary was upstairs resting. Henry and Anne had run out to see Uncle John in the far field; they had seen him mending a fence on the walk home.

"Jane, we've finally had a letter from Father." Mummy was holding it close like precious treasure. It had been a long, long while since they had heard from Father, and every day they stepped forth in faith, hoping for the best, trusting the Lord in light of the worst. "I'd like you to read it."

Jane took the letter carefully and looked at Mummy. She didn't look distressed; rather, she appeared serious. A thinking look, perhaps, encompassed her face. Jane took a deep breath. She would trust and not be afraid. Mummy was entrusting her with Daddy's letter; that was something. She squared her shoulders.

Dear Helen, Jane, and Henry,

I write this letter to you after one of the most dangerous nights I have ever faced. I would be wrong not to say it so. I must write and tell you and also tell of something incredible that happened. I am safe; do not fear. I was spared in the battle, and I know I can only give credit to the Almighty Lord. As a pilot, I face great danger regularly, and I want you to know that, dears—not so you are scared but so you are aware of the great evil we face every day. And I want you to know as each month goes by, the RAF becomes more skilled, more able, more adept.

From the get-go, we were smaller and less trained than Germany, yet we have dominated and turned the tide again and again against the Luftwaffe. I also can only attribute this to God's grace, bringing confusion to the enemy where confusion serves the cause. I've been trained to fly a fighter jet called the Spitfire. Henry, you would be thrilled. It is faster than anything! It can fly over 400 miles per hour. I can't explain how incredible it is. I'm up there, my boy. Flying in the clouds, flying at night by moon and stars, flying in incredible darkness.

    Late in the night, I was facing combat and, more than any other night, fighting fear. The battle was fierce, and for one of the first times, I did worry that my plane was going to go down. I want to write to you, dear ones, so you can know my heart and carry it with you always, no matter what may happen—even though my life was spared.

    I want you to know that alone up there in the dark night skies, out of nowhere, in the midst of great fear, I became suddenly, acutely aware of the Almighty Lord, as if He were right there in the plane with me. In the darkness of the night, when I felt fear creeping in, a passage from

The Lord Is My Light and My Salvation, Whom Shall I Fear?

Psalm 27 came alive in my mind. I had been studying and trying to memorize it during the days at camp because the words would bring me comfort. But I can't explain the way the verses came so clearly alive in my mind on such a deadly night. I can only give credit to our Lord Jesus Christ. I was so strongly aware of His presence. Perhaps you know it? The first bit says, "The Lord is my light and my salvation; whom shall I fear?" The words rolled through my mind like I was viewing them on the page. One line

after the other, bright and clear against darkness.

Helen, everything we've been talking of, writing of, praying about, dear, I think it's all true.

I know it's true.

Tell the children and keep the faith.

I don't have time to write anymore now. I must attend to duties; there is much at hand. Share parts of this with the children as you see fit, Helen. Tell them to write out Scripture to remember it in their hearts. Give them my great love. I am praying for each of you, and when I am alone up in the skies or waiting in transit, I think of you and lift you each to our Good Heavenly Father. I don't know when I'll see you again. But this I do know, and I know for sure: any goodbye here on this earth is not goodbye forever. That's more comfort than I ever thought possible during these dark days. Stay strong, my dears.

All my love,
William (Daddy)

"Oh, Mummy," Jane said. "Do you think Daddy will be okay?"

Jane's mother looked at her straight on. Her

clear eyes held just a bit of shimmer, a witness to the tears held just under the surface. Her young daughter stood before her, growing up before her eyes. Distress was on her face. The war was changing them all. It seemed the children had to grow up faster than ever before. She answered Jane as truthfully as she could. "The truth is, I don't know, Jane, dear. I truly don't know. But we can pray, and we can trust. And Daddy has put his trust in our Merciful Lord, just as you have done, just as I have done." Her smile trembled as Jane looked intently into her face. "And hopefully as Henry has done or will learn to do. We are held in God's love, and that is enough for now."

That night, Jane lay in the dark of her bedroom. She was lost in her thoughts, and fears were insistently knocking when a small voice spoke up out of the darkness.

"Jane?" Anne's voice came across the room.

"Anne? What are you still doing up?" Jane asked, concerned.

"Jane, how do you know God's love is real?" Anne asked in the darkness. Jane thought a moment. She knew the answer was because the Father sent His Son to be the Savior of the world, but that wasn't the answer that sprung first to her lips. She knew Anne's heart was broken in places it might take a long time to mend. She thought about Anne's mum. Anne hadn't heard from her since that letter, so long ago now. She thought about how plucky Anne had been, learning to help in the home and out—and in school, too. So, instead, she started to tell a story.

"Anne, when I think back on the past year and a half or even longer—when I look back even to my days in London before the war, I can see the light of God leading me on and leading me forward, speaking to my heart, and guiding me. One of those steps on the path was coming to Orchard Glen Farm and meeting Uncle John and Aunt Mary. They loved me and Henry with God's love. They love you, too. Do you remember the National Day of Prayer during the time of Dunkirk? I prayed to the

Heavenly Father to be real to me, to help me know His love, and to love Him. I gave Him my heart. Anne, that was one solid step on the path I will never forget." She paused for a moment, thinking. "Now I see Him even more as my Mum has come to know His love." She closed her eyes tight in the darkness to press back tears, swallowed hard and said, "And my Daddy, too. I think if you look back, even though it's hard and even though some things have been bad, I know you'll see His light and love guiding your path, too. And all you have to do is ask. Ask the Almighty Lord to be real to you, to be close to you, to show you His love."

"How'd you ask the Lord to help you know His love, Jane?" Anne's quiet voice floated through the room.

"Why, I just knelt down in the church, 'cause that's where I was at, but you can do this anywhere, and I prayed from my heart to the Lord. God hears our prayers, Anne. And He hears and knows our hearts. Do you remember the hymn 'How Sweet the

Name of Jesus Sounds' that Aunt Mary taught us when you first came? There's a verse in it that goes like this, and I think it's perfect for your question:

By Thee my prayers acceptance gain,
Although with sin defiled;
Satan accuses me in vain,
And I am owned a child."

The room was silent and a heavy, peaceful presence seemed to fill every corner and crevice. Jane noticed she no longer felt afraid.

After a moment, Anne spoke one more time, "Thank you, Jane. I'm glad God put you on my path."

Jane could hear her yawn and shift in the darkness of their room as she rolled over and cuddled down into the blankets.

Jane felt a crackling awareness cover her. What a day this had been.

12

The Notice

Mary's belly was swelling bigger and bigger. It didn't seem possible that she would make it as far into spring as the doctor initially stated. She continued to push back worry and tried to take each day as it came, trusting the Lord. She didn't know it, but Helen, too, was eyeing her warily and keeping a careful eye on her.

Spring had just come to the farm, and there was more work than ever. The children were let off school to help on the farm. The Women's Land Army had come to the village, and every day, wonderful, hardworking women from many English towns and cities were out at all the farms, helping with every farm chore imaginable—from rodent elimination to planting to milking to compost making. Name it and they were doing it with a cheery goodwill that brightened hearts everywhere. Mary was incredibly grateful, grateful for God's provision. What would she do without Helen? John would never have been able to manage without the Land Army. Prime Minister Churchill continued to rally the people and state that the home front battle was the most important. Everything must be done to keep Germany from starving out England and destroying the country from the inside out. So far, it was working. Mary tried not to panic. Her emotions seemed to run high, and anything could set off a bout of tears. That would never do. The uncertainties would not get the better of her. She placed her hand on her belly. My, there was a lot of baby in there. She tried hard each day to treasure the gift of this new life despite all the physical discomfort, and she did seem to have so much of that. For one moment, she sat and took time to thank the Lord for His care of her, for this new life, for the absolute wonder of a new baby, for the people He had placed around her in so many ways. She thought of Mary, the mother of Jesus, and her sweet, wholehearted surrender to the Lord, "Be it done to me according to Your will." *Let my heart be like Mary's, Lord. Help me to know You in the surrender.* She closed her eyes in a heartfelt prayer.

Mary hoisted herself up out of the chair and stepped out into the kitchen to wash some dishes. A cramping pain seized her back and she bit her lip. Surely it wasn't time. She put her hand on the small of her back and leaned over a bit. She and John had made a plan for how to handle the baby's birth. If at all possible, she would be at home with the midwife and Helen attending. John would take the children out to the fields and orchard with him, checking back every now and again to see if anything was needed. She had everything set for the baby's birth. Her thoughts were cut off by the loud rumble of a motorcar coming down the road.

"Who could that be?" she wondered aloud and looked out the door. She felt alarmed when she saw a uniformed officer stepping out of the car, and then another cramp, a bit firmer, like a fist, began to roll out over her back. She had to call for Helen. Quickly, she started praying for peace, for protection, for comfort, for everything she could think of and anything she couldn't: *Merciful Lord, help us all.*

"Helen?" She leaned out the kitchen door toward the herb garden. Helen was out there planting some seeds. "I think there's an officer here to see you." Helen stood up and all the color drained from her face in one instant. She swayed a bit. Wiping her hands on her apron, she started walking toward the house in a daze.

Mary grabbed her arm and walked with her around the house to the door where the officer stood.

The Notice

"Mrs. Townsend?" The officer looked from Helen to Mary, not knowing who was who. Meanwhile, Mary was heroically trying to manage another wave of pain so no one would know what was possibly happening.

"Yes, that's me," poor Helen managed to choke out.

"I've a notice for you here from the RAF. It's an urgent matter." The officer handed her the note and then turned to walk back to his car. Helen and Mary stood staring after him, unable to utter a single word.

"I don't think it's the worst, Helen. He wouldn't have walked away," Mary said carefully through gritted teeth. Helen stood frozen, holding the notice. She shook her head briskly.

"You're right. But I don't know what it could be. Why, Mary, what's the matter?" Mary could hardly stand up straight.

"Oh, Helen, I think it might be time for the baby."

Helen took one good, clear look at Mary, the first clear look she had really taken all day. "Why yes, dear, I think you're right. Let's get you into the house. I'll run to get John to send for the midwife." Helen had Mary by the elbow and was gently steering her forward, the notice gripped in her other hand.

"Open the letter, Helen. Let's face this head-on first," Mary urged desperately.

Helen stopped. Open the notice? The letter that could change her life forever? She gulped.

"Go on," Mary whispered.

"All right," Helen's voice was barely there. With a deep breath, she ripped the notice open and forced herself to read.

Suddenly and dramatically, she burst into tears. Mary didn't know what to do. The pain was starting to get a bit desperate in this standing, upright position. Was William dead? She gritted her teeth and waited.

After a moment, Helen managed to say, "Oh,

The Notice

Mary, William's alive! He was shot down in combat but not captured. He's broken both an arm and a leg and is being sent here to Orchard Glen Farm to recover. He might never go back to flying again."

"Why, Helen, I'm so glad. So glad." Mary forgot herself for a moment in the joy for Helen. "So glad." Relief that William was actually alive and would recover flooded both women. All would be well. All would be well at Orchard Glen Farm and for the people sheltered under the cover of God's love and within its enduring walls. Mary tried to smile and speak again but gasped instead and bent over.

"Oh my, what a day already," Helen said crisply as her attention diverted to Mary with laser-like focus. Relief for William filled her whole being; even she hadn't realized how much she was dreading a notice of terrible news. William was injured, again, but he would recover. Tears of joy sprang to her eyes. Quickly, she jumped back into action. Mary really needed her. In no time, Mary was situated, the midwife was on the way, and the children were securely away with John, bubbling over with excitement that the baby was actually coming.

Someone new would be at Orchard Glen Farm shortly. Helen grinned. A little boy or a little girl? She couldn't wait to find out. She tucked the notice in a safe place as she bustled about the kitchen, getting everything sorted. She had to remember to tell Jane and Henry that Daddy would be coming to the farm to stay.

13

God Moves in a Mysterious Way, His Wonders to Perform

The afternoon sunlight puddled around Mary as she sat in the rocking chair with not one, but two babies tucked under her chin. That day, the day of the fateful notice and their birth, was a hazy blur. Her feet pounded a gentle, but relentless, rocking rhythm. Even more now, than ever, was she thankful for Helen and the Lord's great provision at Orchard Glen Farm. She sighed gratefully. My, she was tired. Tired in a different way, tired in a new way, tired in a *twin* way. The babies snuggled together in a bassinet, their velvet heads swaddled perfectly by warm blankets. Her heart was full—full because of these beloved, precious bundles. Suddenly, she pressed back tears of gratitude. After so long, and such longing, she and John had not one precious baby, but two darling baby girls: Grace Elizabeth and Joy Abigail. She began to sing a bit as she rocked, favorite hymns, one after the other.

John was watching her from the doorway. Her gold head glinted in the mellow afternoon light.

Two little bundles were tightly swaddled and tucked up under her chin. She didn't look half as exhausted as she would have if not for Helen, Jane, and Anne. He still stood amazed at the way circumstances played out all around him. William had arrived back at the farm and was mending, and what a good head for problem solving he had. It was mighty helpful to talk over farm problems with him and figure out solutions.

Mary turned her head and saw John standing in the doorway. "Why, John, I didn't know you were there," she called out softly, so as not to wake the babes.

John crossed the room to her, his heart full of the blessed abundances born during the time of suffering and war, tucked up in her arms, rocking in this chair. Surely, God moves in a mysterious way, His wonders to perform.

"Ah, Mary, I just came to check on you and see if anything was needed." John's low rumble echoed through the room. The babies didn't stir at all, his voice as familiar to them as their mother's heartbeat.

"I'm doing just fine; the girls take such good care of me. Did you know that Susan, from the WI, stopped by and brought canned goods and linens and other supplies? She even brought two hand-knit blankets for the babies that she made herself. She stacked everything up on the kitchen table for us to sort through. Such goodness there. So kind of them all."

"Aye, I saw a stack in the kitchen," John said with a twinkle in his eye. "I didn't know that came from the WI." Mary looked at him. John knew that look, and he laughed out loud. "No worries, Mary, love. I'll have it sorted and put away in no time. We are so blessed." This part he said with all seriousness.

Because they were.

Outside the front of the house, Helen stood next to her beloved William. He was leaning on his crutch heavily, and as she stood next to him, they leaned into each other. William was already a

God Moves in a Mysterious Way, His Wonders to Perform

help on the farm, with his quick, intelligent mind, but it would be many weeks before he was able to physically be out and about, handling the labor so desperately needed at Orchard Glen Farm. He would regain his strength. With the Lord's help, the fresh English air, and the nourishment from Orchard Glen Farm—before too long, he would be shouldering the work at hand with mind and with body.

"Look at that expanse of sky," William said quietly. The afternoon light was turning, and everything was rimmed in gold.

"It's beautiful here. There's a part of me that doesn't ever want to leave," Helen admitted quietly. "There's just something in the country air. I'm not quite sure what it is."

"So many days lie ahead with so much uncertainty. This war is far from over," William said.

Helen shuddered a bit. She knew that to be truer than she could understand. "We can take it one day at a time, trusting the Lord. Here, at Orchard Glen Farm. It's all we can do, with everything changing sometimes by the hour. Day by day and one moment at a time." Her gentle words were filled with hard-won courage, and William knew them to ring true.

"Yes. One day at a time." William turned to her with a smile in his eyes and on his face.

"Here, at Orchard Glen Farm."

Jane and Henry and Anne were together in the orchard. Helen had sent them out with a picnic basket and a large blanket. They had spread the blanket out upon the ground and were lying on their backs looking up at the sky. They looked like stair steps lying there. First, Jane. Then, Henry. And then, Anne. One black head and one blond and one honeyed brown, shining in the afternoon light. They were cloud watching and trying to guess what shapes and animals they could see in the cloud puffs floating in the sky above their heads. The sky was turning pink and gold.

Jane thought about everything that had happened since she stepped on the train with Henry so long ago. It was too much to fathom. She thought about Aunt Mary holding her two baby girls. The look in Uncle John's eyes. Why, the look in Mother's. Jane sometimes caught her staring at Daddy when she thought no one was watching; she looked at him like she would never let him out of her sight again. Jane thought about Daddy and all the pain he was in and the way his faith in the Heavenly Father seemed to drive away any bitterness or fear. Jane turned her head and looked at Henry and Anne. They were good-naturedly arguing over whether the cloud directly over their heads looked like a lion or a cheetah.

"He has a mane!" Henry insisted.

"Look at those long cheetah legs," Anne countered. Then they both laughed, for the cloud dissipated and split apart, and nothing was recognizable anymore. They were happy and carefree and healthy and pink-cheeked.

Jane turned her head back and looked straight up at the sky with gray eyes firm in gaze and strong in courage. She didn't know how much longer the war would go on, but this one thing she knew—and her heart swelled with joy—they would all be together, safe at Orchard Glen Farm.

14

Orchard Glen Farm Forever

A few weeks later, Helen and Jane were busy working together to bathe the twins while Anne helped by running small errands and standing by with towels and nappies. Looking over her shoulder, with a slippery baby in a firm grasp, Helen encouraged Jane who was trying to bathe Joy, "That's right, my girl. Keep a firm but gentle grip and make sure to support her head." Baby Joy scrunched up her tiny face and let out a little wail. She was not fond of the water at all. Jane looked worried, and Helen laughed. "She's all right. It takes a bit for some babies to get used to their bath." Baby Grace, on the other hand, was resting in the water peacefully in Helen's hands. Anne held two towels in her arms and watched with wide eyes. Jane seemed to be getting the knack of it. Sometimes, when the babies cried a lot, she and Jane would sit together, one on each side of a cradle, and help Aunt Mary by gently rocking them. Anne enjoyed that, but she was in no hurry to hold a slippery baby.

 Mary had just stepped outside to get a breath of fresh air and clear her mind. The babies were going through a growth spurt and eating constantly. She inhaled deeply and smiled. It was beyond lovely to have the love and friendship and support of the Townsends and sweet Anne at Orchard Glen Farm. She looked across the field and saw John heading toward her. He seemed to have some purpose in mind. She walked toward him and met him as he came across the front path.

"We've 'ad a letter from Anne's mum, Mary," he said quietly as he greeted her. "She's asked us to keep Anne for good."

Mary stared at John, stunned for a minute. It wasn't terribly unusual for evacuees to rehome during wartimes. Sometimes it happened, particularly in situations like Anne's. Yet, Mary hadn't dared hope that the sweet, honey-haired darling could actually be hers. She had tried to carefully walk the fine balance of loving her but helping her keep a right heart toward her mum. Inside, she had struggled. Sometimes, she felt angry. She hurt with the little girl's confusion and heartache. Her heart welled with hope, but before she could say anything in return, John continued.

"And Mary, I'd like to ask William and Helen to stay on at the farm, for good. We've got the summer house over there past the pastures. I don't think it'll take much to situate it into a real home for their family. I know William will help me work on it soon as he's fully mended. No rush, but I know they'd prefer a place of their own. They've lost their place in London, and there's no flyin' for William now. They've been such a help and comfort. I feel they belong here. Helen helps so much with the twins, and there's so much work on the farm. Why, she's practically a member of the Women's Land Army with all she does 'round here." He laughed. "And I've never 'ad such help as William gives. He 'as the sharpest mind I've ever known."

"Why, John," Mary said, "nothing could make me happier. I don't know what I'd do without those children. And Helen, why, she's become such a dear friend. Helen hasn't said much, but I know the loss of their London home and all the uncertainty has been weighing heavy on her heart."

"Let's speak to them privately; be sure it's what they all want," John said.

Later that day, Jane and Henry learned from Mum and Dad that they would be staying on at Orchard Glen Farm, for good. Jane had squealed, and Henry had whooped. They had run out to the orchard and spun around and around for joy. They could scarcely believe it. Dad had looked so happy, and Mummy, too. They sat down next to their favorite tree and talked over all that would be now that Orchard Glen Farm was their place forever.

Anne, too, had a private and very gentle talk with Aunt Mary. Orchard Glen Farm would be her home—and more than that, Anne would be Aunt Mary's very own and belong to her for always. She slipped away with shining eyes and found Jane and Henry in the orchard. The three joined hands and twirled around until they fell to the ground, breathless and laughing.

That night, everyone was at the table; Mary had baby Grace nestled in her arms, and John held Joy. Anne was next to Mary, and Jane and Henry were between Helen and William. Mary's candles seemed to flicker with extra liveliness, their gold glimmer lighting all the faces around the table and shining against the familiar red-checked tablecloth.

Jane and Henry: A World War II Adventure: A Sequel

Mary and John looked out at their full table: Jane, Henry, Anne, Helen, William, and, unbelievably, their own twins in their arms. Their hearts overflowed. Sometimes, dreams do come true.

"Let's pray," said Uncle John, and the joy in his voice filled the room.

Appendix

Uncle John's Christmas Nativity Program

The readings can be broken up over the time leading up to Christmas, used as a portion of Advent celebrations, or enjoyed during the week between Christmas and Epiphany (the 12th day after Christmas when some Christians remember the Wise Men).

Matthew 1:18
Now the birth of Jesus Christ was on this wise: When as his mother Mary was espoused to Joseph, before they came together, she was found with child of the Holy Ghost.

It happened like this:
Luke 1:26–40

And in the sixth month the angel Gabriel was sent from God unto a city of Galilee, named Nazareth,

To a virgin espoused to a man whose name was Joseph, of the house of David; and the virgin's name was Mary.

And the angel came in unto her, and said, Hail, thou that art highly favoured, the Lord is with thee: blessed art thou among women.

And when she saw him, she was troubled at his saying, and cast in her mind what manner of salutation this should be.

And the angel said unto her, Fear not, Mary: for thou hast found favour with God.

And, behold, thou shalt conceive in thy womb, and bring forth a son, and shalt call his name Jesus. He shall be great, and shall be called the Son of the Highest: and the Lord God shall give unto him the throne of his father David:

And he shall reign over the house of Jacob for ever; and of his kingdom there shall be no end.

Then said Mary unto the angel, How shall this be,

seeing I know not a man?

And the angel answered and said unto her, The Holy Ghost shall come upon thee, and the power of the Highest shall overshadow thee: therefore also that holy thing which shall be born of thee shall be called the Son of God.

And, behold, thy cousin Elisabeth, she hath also conceived a son in her old age: and this is the sixth month with her, who was called barren.

For with God nothing shall be impossible.

And Mary said, Behold the handmaid of the Lord; be it unto me according to thy word. And the angel departed from her.

And Mary arose in those days, and went into the hill country with haste, into a city of Juda;

And entered into the house of Zacharias, and saluted Elisabeth.

Luke 1:56

And Mary abode with her about three months, and returned to her own house.

Place stable and manger.

Luke 2:1–38

And it came to pass in those days, that there went out a decree from Caesar Augustus that all the world should be taxed.

(And this taxing was first made when Cyrenius was governor of Syria.)

And all went to be taxed, every one into his own city.

And Joseph also went up from Galilee, out of the city of Nazareth, into Judaea, unto the city of David, which is called Bethlehem; (because he was of the house and lineage of David:)

To be taxed with Mary his espoused wife, being great with child.

And so it was, that, while they were there, the days were accomplished that she should be delivered.

And she brought forth her firstborn son, and wrapped him in swaddling clothes, and laid him in a manger; because there was no room for them in the inn.

Place donkey, Mary, Joseph, and baby Jesus in the manger.

Place oxen and/or cow and goat if available.

And there were in the same country shepherds abiding in the field, keeping watch over their flock by night.

And, lo, the angel of the Lord came upon them, and the glory of the Lord shone round about them: and they were sore afraid.

And the angel said unto them, Fear not: for, behold, I bring you good tidings of great joy, which shall be to all people.

For unto you is born this day in the city of David a Saviour, which is Christ the Lord.

And this shall be a sign unto you; Ye shall find the babe wrapped in swaddling clothes, lying in a manger.

And suddenly there was with the angel a multitude of the heavenly host praising God, and saying,

Glory to God in the highest, and on earth peace,

good will toward men.

Place angel(s) near Mary.

And it came to pass, as the angels were gone away from them into heaven, the shepherds said one to another, Let us now go even unto Bethlehem, and see this thing which is come to pass, which the Lord hath made known unto us.

And they came with haste, and found Mary, and Joseph, and the babe lying in a manger.

And when they had seen it, they made known abroad the saying which was told them concerning this child.

And all they that heard it wondered at those things which were told them by the shepherds.

Place shepherds and sheep.

But Mary kept all these things, and pondered them in her heart.

And the shepherds returned, glorifying and praising God for all the things that they had heard and seen, as it was told unto them.

And when eight days were accomplished for the circumcising of the child, his name was called Jesus, which was so named of the angel before he was conceived in the womb.

And when the days of her purification according to the law of Moses were accomplished, they brought him to Jerusalem, to present him to the Lord;

(As it is written in the law of the Lord, Every male that openeth the womb shall be called holy to the Lord;)

And to offer a sacrifice according to that which is said in the law of the Lord, A pair of turtledoves, or two young pigeons.

And, behold, there was a man in Jerusalem, whose name was Simeon; and the same man was just and devout, waiting for the consolation of Israel: and the Holy Ghost was upon him.

And it was revealed unto him by the Holy Ghost,

that he should not see death, before he had seen the Lord's Christ.

And he came by the Spirit into the temple: and when the parents brought in the child Jesus, to do for him after the custom of the law,

Then took he him up in his arms, and blessed God, and said,

Lord, now lettest thou thy servant depart in peace, according to thy word:

For mine eyes have seen thy salvation,

Which thou hast prepared before the face of all people;

A light to lighten the Gentiles, and the glory of thy people Israel.

And Joseph and his mother marvelled at those things which were spoken of him.

And Simeon blessed them, and said unto Mary his mother, Behold, this child is set for the fall and rising again of many in Israel; and for a sign which shall be spoken against;

(Yea, a sword shall pierce through thy own soul

also,) that the thoughts of many hearts may be revealed.

And there was one Anna, a prophetess, the daughter of Phanuel, of the tribe of Aser: she was of a great age, and had lived with an husband seven years from her virginity;

And she was a widow of about fourscore and four years, which departed not from the temple, but served God with fastings and prayers night and day.

And she coming in that instant gave thanks likewise unto the Lord, and spake of him to all them that looked for redemption in Jerusalem.

Matthew 2:1–12

Now when Jesus was born in Bethlehem of Judaea in the days of Herod the king, behold, there came wise men from the east to Jerusalem, saying, Where is he that is born King of the Jews? for we have seen his star in the east, and are come to worship him.

When Herod the king had heard these things, he was troubled, and all Jerusalem with him.

And when he had gathered all the chief priests and scribes of the people together, he demanded of them where Christ should be born.

And they said unto him, In Bethlehem of Judaea: for thus it is written by the prophet,

And thou Bethlehem, in the land of Juda, art not the least among the princes of Juda: for out of thee shall come a Governor, that shall rule my people Israel.

Then Herod, when he had privily called the wise men, enquired of them diligently what time the star appeared.

And he sent them to Bethlehem, and said, Go and search diligently for the young child; and when ye have found him, bring me word again, that I may come and worship him also.

When they had heard the king, they departed; and, lo, the star, which they saw in the east, went before them, till it came and stood over where the young child was.

When they saw the star, they rejoiced with exceeding great joy.

And when they were come into the house, they saw the young child with Mary his mother, and fell down, and worshipped him: and when they had opened their treasures, they presented unto him gifts; gold, frankincense, and myrrh.

And being warned of God in a dream that they should not return to Herod, they departed into their own country another way.

Place magi and camel.

Luke 2:39–40

And when they had performed all things according to the law of the Lord, they returned into Galilee, to their own city Nazareth.

And the child grew, and waxed strong in spirit, filled with wisdom: and the grace of God was upon him.

Sing the lively *Sussex Carol,* which is a traditional English Christmas carol:

Appendix

1. *On Christmas night all Christians sing*
To hear the news the angels bring
(repeat lines one and two).
News of great joy, news of great mirth,
News of our merciful King's birth.

2. *Then why should men on earth be so sad,*
Since our Redeemer made us glad
(repeat lines one and two),
When from our sin he set us free,
All for to gain our liberty?

3. *When sin departs before His grace,*
Then life and health come in its place
(repeat lines one and two).
Angels and men with joy may sing
All for to see the new-born King.

4. *All out of darkness we have light,*
Which made the angels sing this night
(repeat lines one and two):

"Glory to God and peace to men,
Now and for evermore, Amen!"

Winston Churchill

Winston Churchill was the Prime Minister of England from 1940–1945 and again from 1951–1955; he is renowned for leading Britain to victory during World War II. Widely regarded for his incredible rhetorical and persuasive speeches, his words can be found online, both in writing and audio/video recordings. He gave four of his most famous speeches during 1940, the context of this story and *Jane and Henry: A World War II Adventure*. *Jane and Henry: A World War II Adventure* refers to the speech titled "This Was Their Finest Hour," in which Churchill declares the Battle of Britain is about to begin, while this story references "The Few," which has an incredible passage praising the pilots of the Royal Air Force. Finally, "We Shall Fight on the Beaches" is the speech Churchill

Appendix

delivered after the miraculous Dunkirk evacuation, an event referenced in *Jane and Henry: A World War II Adventure*. Churchill's speeches are a marvel and worthy of appreciation.

The four speeches referenced are as follows:

"Blood, Toil, Tears, and Sweat"—May 10, 1940

"We Shall Fight on the Beaches"—June 4, 1940

"This Was Their Finest Hour"—June 18, 1940

"The Few"—August 20, 1940

More books from The Good and the Beautiful Library

The Story of Louis Pasteur
by Alida Sims Malkus

Brian's Victory
by Ethel Calvert Phillips

Cherokee Run
by Barbara Smucker

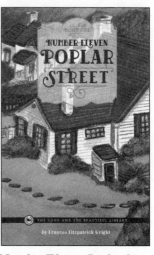

Number Eleven Poplar Street
by Frances Fitzpatrick Wright

goodandbeautiful.com